BULL TRAINS
to
DEADWOOD

BULL TRAINS
to
DEADWOOD

CHUCK CECIL

Published by The History Press
Charleston, SC
www.historypress.com

Cover image courtesy of the South Dakota Historical Society.

First published 2020

Manufactured in the United States

ISBN 9781467144223

Library of Congress Control Number: 2019951977

CONTENTS

ACKNOWLEDGEMENTS

MY THANKS FOR ALL THE HELP

I was scrubbing a century's worth of Dakota dust off of a dried-up, old ox yoke in preparation for a display in the Brookings County Museum in Volga, South Dakota, where I'm a volunteer. As I worked on the yoke, which was worn for a dozen years by Pete and Luke, loyal oxen owned by homesteader Peter Haas in the 1870s, I wondered about ox yokes and the animals that wore them. This moment led me to read thousands of old and frayed newspapers and books, and it allowed me to meet a freight wagon–load of good and helpful people who responded to my inane questions and pointed me in the right direction when I veered off track.

I would especially like to thank Lonis Wendt of Vivian, South Dakota, who knows the two hundred-mile wagon road from Fort Pierre to Deadwood like the back of his hand. He's walked it and bumped along it in his pickup. Along with a few other amateur South Dakota historians, Lonis is an expert on the history of the road and the times when it was a veritable superhighway for bull trains and other beasts of burden lugging goods to the remote Black Hills.

I'm also grateful for my daughter, Amy Cecil Holm, who would grab my manuscript and make it better even after she had been grading her college students' essays late into the night.

I would like to give a big thank-you to Doug Hansen, who envisioned and then developed Hansen Wheel and Wagon Shop near Letcher, South Dakota. His leadership has brought the shop to a world-class status among makers of all sorts of old horse-drawn wagons and conveyances, including the beer wagons and stagecoaches you've probably seen in television commercials. Doug is an "old wagon" expert, and with his talented craftsmen, he has made and restored hundreds of other wooden-wheeled masterpieces.

Betsy Lenning of the public library in Brookings, South Dakota, was always there to help me and order miles and miles of old newspaper microfilm. At the South Dakota State University Archives, Crystal Gamradt and Ruby Wilson came through when I wanted to learn something about oxen, wagons or how much it cost in 1878 or 1886 to ship one hundred pounds of flour from Pierre to Deadwood.

I would also like to give my sincere thanks to Tom Munson of the Sioux City Public Museum; Rick Mills of the South Dakota State Railroad Museum, Ltd., in Hill City; Matthew Reitzel of the South Dakota State Historical Society; Mark Slocum of the Minnilusa Historical Association in Rapid City; and Troy Kilpatrick of the Journey Museum, which is also in Rapid City.

My kid brother Bob Cecil was always there when I needed pictures. His daughter Darsha of Spearfish, South Dakota, also helped me in this area, as she is also an accomplished photographer.

Sizi Taylor at the Wyoming State Archives searched diligently for pictures in her state's vast vault of photographs, as did Hannah Marshall at Deadwood Histories, Inc., and I am grateful for them.

My thanks also go out to Rolland Johnson for his oxen insights. As a young man, Johnson got into the radio business, and before he retired to his Three Eagles Ranch along the Palmer Divide southeast of Larkspur, Colorado, he had acquired and improved on dozens of radio stations in several midwestern states. As a hobby, Rollie and his wife, Paula, started raising Milking Devon cattle as oxen. The couple trained the oxen, showed them and came to love and respect them.

I would also like to thank Dr. Andrew Conroy, a professor of animal science at the University of New Hampshire who also knows oxen; Katie Hunhoff and her staff who create the excellent *South Dakota* magazine in Yankton; and to all others the who, in big and small ways, helped me get to know more about oxen, freight wagons and the Fort Pierre to Deadwood Trail.

—Chuck Cecil

1

THE GOLD

Eight hundred ounces of gold dust arrived in this city today. Yesterday, a solid piece of quartz was consigned to the Pacific Coast for exhibition, which bristles with free gold all over. The piece weighs about twenty-five pounds and is estimated to contain a hundred dollars of gold. This is from the Alpha Mine, and specimens of the same ore [are] *now exhibited in Philadelphia in the name of W.C. Bennet.*
—Press and Dakotian, *Yankton, Dakota Territory, August 26, 1876*

xperienced miners who accompanied George Armstrong Custer's Black Hills Expedition found gold in 1874. The Seventh Cavalry's impetuous commander's announcement of its existence sparked a whirlwind across the land. Custer penned General Phil Sheridan about the find from his elaborate Black Hills Expedition command tent, which sat on the banks of French Creek. "I have here, lying before me, forty or fifty small particles of pure gold—most of it obtained from one pan full of earth."

Custer's glowing report, along with other accounts from the newspapermen who accompanied his command, triggered the most memorable gold rush in American history. The news and consequential follow-up from the government scientists who were assigned to verify the French Creek find captured a nation that was weary from the Civil War and its aftermath. Thousands of war veterans and other adventurous men and women were financially drained by the depressing shenanigans of 1873, which were fueled by colossal business failures and grasshopper- and drought-ravaged crops in the Midwest. These three million idle souls, who were out of money and close to giving up, read that the Black Hills contained gold in prolific amounts—some of it even clinging to the roots of beets growing in a Deadwood garden. Thousands of people packed their duffels and headed for the isolated and beautiful Black Hills in the southwest corner of the Dakota Territory.

Before Custer's discovery, the Black Hills were just curiosities in the center of the nation; they were largely unexplored, crudely mapped and mostly unknown. All of that changed in the mid-1870s, as Custer and his cavalry were riding back to Fort Abraham Lincoln in the Northern Dakota Territory. Everyone wanted to learn more about the rugged, inaccessible and mysterious place that had been claimed a century earlier by the Sioux. The Sioux leaders and the Black Hills characters that emerged during the mad scramble to that sacred, golden ground are, to this day, either glamorized or vilified. Names like Red Cloud, Spotted Tail, Sitting Bull, Calamity Jane, Persimmons Bill Chambers, Preacher Smith, Wild Bill Hickok and others captured the nation's imagination. They became iconic frontier figures and remain so today. No other American gold rush has inspired such a lasting interest.

For millions of years, the gold in the Black Hills was squeezed away in rocky crags—its gold-specked veins packed and sealed tightly in strata of quartz between mountains of granite that had erupted from the bowels of the earth. Some of that gold was leeched away during periodic tectonic tantrums and earthly hiccups and emerged as glistening specks, odd-shaped flakes and gleaming nuggets that all settled on the flood banks and sandy beds of the streams that rippled down the steep, pine-clad canyons. One of those streams would become known as French Creek and as the place where Lieutenant Colonel George Custer's fame took a turn from his Civil War exploits. The gold in the Black Hills sparked another war that burst forth on the territory's endless and semiarid prairie.

Custer's journey to the Black Hills commenced on a hot July 2 in 1874. It was a seemingly innocent trek, publicly advertised as an excursion to locate potential sites for army outposts. But a few high-ranking officials in the government were also silently hoping that gold would be found there, as its presence had been rumored for years by a few who claimed to have secretly mined small fortunes in those distant hills. According to Herbert Schell's book *South Dakota: Its Beginnings and Growth*, Lieutenant Colonel Custer and about one thousand Seventh Cavalry troopers escorting more than one hundred rattling supply and ambulance wagons shoved off from Fort Abraham Lincoln near what is now Bismarck, North Dakota. They left

Lieutenant Colonel George Custer's Seventh Cavalry heads out on the 1874 Black Hills Expedition, which was more than two hundred miles from their home base at Fort Abraham Lincoln, Dakota Territory. Part of the reason for the expedition into Sioux lands was to determine whether there was gold in the hills. This photo, by expedition photographer W.H. Illingworth of St. Paul, shows the four-column march near what is today the North Dakota and South Dakota border. *South Dakota State Historical Society.*

a cloud of Dakota roiling dust in their wake, and their course was set for the dark and sacred Sioux land full of dense pine trees that soon appeared on the far horizon as a black mass framed with billowing white clouds. The Sioux called the place Paha Sapa (Black Hills). Spirits lived there, and those spirits kindly allowed their worshipers to enter the pines on brief hunting forays and to harvest strong, straight lodge poles for tepees.

After eighteen days, Custer's soldiers were energized by the sight of the black mass of mountains in the distance; they were still a two-day march away. In four columns, the cavalry arrived at the northern foothills and casually rode along the Black Hills' western edge before locating a wagon-friendly opening into the hills' beautiful park-like interior. Custer and a few others took some time to climb what is now known as Black Elk Peak (once Harney Peak). At 7,241 feet, it has been described as the highest peak in the nation east of the Rocky Mountains. Impressed with the beauty and serenity of the hills, Custer's command camped along French Creek near what became the city of Custer. The town that sprouted there was named in honor of Custer for his Civil War exploits, not the historic Black Hills odyssey he undertook. Over the next several idyllic days along French Creek, gold was found in paying amounts.

Thirty-two-year-old trusted scout, guide, and eastern college dropout Charley Reynolds was the messenger that Custer selected to carry the golden news back to civilization. Reynolds rode on his horse with muffled hooves in order to mute the sound and disguise the trail; he rode for four nights—hiding and resting during the day—through Sioux country to deliver Custer's letter and the newspaper reporters' stories to Fort Laramie, Wyoming Territory, which was 150 miles away. Custer's message and the newspaper accounts were tapped out to the world over telegraph wires. One of the reporters with Custer was *Chicago Inter-Ocean* correspondent William E. Curtis. In his communiqué, dated August 27, 1884, he wrote that the expedition "will carry back the news that there is gold here, in quantities as rich as were ever dreamed." Later, in August 1874, the *Chicago Inter-Ocean* published at the top of its front page a crudely drawn map of the Dakota Territory and the Black Hills. The map was carefully torn away and tucked into the shirt pockets of gold-seekers who were heading west for their fortunes.

While the discovery was news to a vast majority of people, it wasn't for the few hunters, trappers and traders who claimed to have known about the hidden treasures in the forbidden hills for years. At that time, their reports of gold had not been officially authenticated; it was Custer's lot to do that. Ironically, Custer and many of his cavalry troops would pay with their lives for the news of gold, which ultimately led to the nation's impotence in enforcing the earlier Laramie Treaty obligations with the Sioux. These treaty violations understandably did not sit well with Sitting Bull, Spotted Tail and the other leaders of the vast Sioux Nation. Two years after Custer's Black Hills Expedition, the whirlwind he had unleashed spun out of control and came tumbling down around him and his Seventh Cavalry troops on the Greasy Grass in the Montana Territory in what became known as the Battle of Little Bighorn. Even after the battle, the national press fanned the golden flames daily. On July 2, 1876, the territory's capital city newspaper, the *Yankton Press and Dakotian*, reported:

> *Private advices from the Black Hills Expedition received this morning show that investigations are proving the country to be richer in gold than has previously been supposed. The earth down to bed rock in every direction is filled with particles of gold, and the quartz shows rich veins.*

On his return trip from the Black Hills, Custer (*seated in the center of the photograph behind the bear*) shot this old six-hundred-pound male grizzly bear on August 6, 1884, using his .50-caliber Remington sporting rifle. Custer's main scout, Bloody Knife, is seated behind him to his right. Private Noonan is standing to Custer's left and behind Captain William Ludlow. One of Custer's hounds sleeps contentedly behind the bear, on the far left of the photograph. *South Dakota State Historical Society.*

The following month, in August 1876, the *Yankton Press and Dakotian*, the territory's most influential newspaper, printed a story that said a nugget taken from Custer's Gulch had been valued at $18. The story also noted that $50 of gold per day had been taken from the gulch, and the paper reprinted news from Deadwood's *Black Hills Pioneer* newspaper about the arrival of eight hundred ounces of gold dust in town. On September 28, 1876, the

Yankton paper said that a party of local miners had brought home Black Hills gold that was valued at $40,000—equivalent to about $900,000 today.

Gold news continued to spew over the land. The news was made even more inviting to fortune hunters when more gold was found in abundance in Deadwood Gulch, which was just a couple days walk from the Custer Expedition's French Creek findings. The thousands of miners that were said to have been living in Custer packed up and headed for the gulch and newfound bonanza. The tiny camp called Deadwood soon became a crowded, raucous, magical place where miners and hangers-on flocked to find their fortune. For the remainder of the gold rush, the area within ten or fifteen miles of Deadwood was a busy trade center.

Nearby, in Lead City, the Homestake Mine, which soon became the world's largest and deepest gold mine, was discovered in April 1876. Miners continued to dig for gold there until 2002, and in that area, modern miners still find the magic metal today. In 2017, the Wharf Mine, which is also in the Lead area, yielded 95,372 ounces of gold, according to a report in the *Rapid City Journal* in February 2019. Other minerals are probably still embedded in the strata of the Black Hills. On March 15, 1875, the *New York Times* reported that the hills also contained massive gypsum deposits, silver, graphite, lead, fuller's earth, volcanic ash, coal, cement, copper, nickel, iron and tin.

Miners, businessmen, farmers, ranchers, camp followers and an army of miscreants and scofflaws gathered in milling crowds at the railroad towns that were as close as possible to the isolated Black Hills at that time: Sidney, Nebraska (270 miles north of the Union Pacific's tracks); Cheyenne in the Wyoming Territory (nearly 300 miles from the same railroad's tracks); Yankton in Southeastern Dakota Territory (250 miles away); and Bismarck (far north of where the Northern Pacific railroad could drop off miners 245 miles from the Black Hills).

The *Yankton Press and Dakotian* reported in August 1876, "A large party will leave Yankton for the Black Hills. A party from Wisconsin will also leave today and join the Yankton party. The train will consist of some ten or fifteen wagons. The party is well-outfitted and well-armed." In April 1877, the newspaper reported, "The Dakota Central [Railroad] brought three coaches containing two hundred Black Hillers." Two days later, the same newspaper reported, "About four hundred men arrived on last night's train from Sioux City, mostly [bound] for the Black Hills." In its March 5 edition, the newspaper reported, "Thirty men from Dubuque [Iowa] will arrive this week en route to the Black Hills."

Mining and camping equipment—mostly placer pans, shovels, and pickaxes—was gathered up. Rifles were cleaned and pistols were holstered. Information about the overland travel routes was penciled in, and trips were sketched out on the fragile map from the *Inter-Ocean News*. The book *Guide to the Black Hills* by Edwin Curley was a popular purchase. Curley listed what miners headed for the hills would need, and he advised everyone to use care in dealings with Hillers (white men who might take advantage of new arrivals to the Black Hills); the book warned arrivals to beware of "tricks that are vain." Most dream-seekers headed for Deadwood, the spinning hub of the golden excitement; the famous town grew to a population of five thousand almost overnight. It was a lawless place; a gun was judge and jury. Between November 15, 1875, and March 1, 1876, an estimated ten thousand people arrived in the eight thousand square miles of the Black Hills. Five years later, the area's population would be around twenty thousand, according to the *Black Hills Daily Times* on February 23, 1884. But the Laramie Treaty soon became a problem.

The Black Hills, and the land over which the miners and other settlers had to travel, did not belong to the United States. Everyone traveling to the Black Hills, and those already in the Black Hills, were trespassing on a sovereign nation's land and illegally removing its resources. After Custer's 1874 expedition, this presence of United States citizens in the Black Hills became a problem for the federal government. Try as government forces might, it was impossible to turn back and eject the determined masses clawing and clamoring for gold. For the government to send home those who were already in the Black Hills and to slam the door on those who were on their way was impractical. The hills were like the hub of a gigantic wagon wheel, with supporting spokes all around. The relatively small contingent of soldiers at Fort Laramie, which was more than 150 miles away from the Black Hills, tried to stop the rush, but with a trip of several days between them and the hills and the amount of supplies they would need to maintain a sizeable force there for weeks, it was an impossible task.

There already existed three roads and trails across the Sioux land that had been approved by the tribe in the Laramie Treaty. The treaty also allowed railroad surveyors and construction workers to enter tribal land. Gold-seekers were not included on the list of approved visitors, but how could anyone tell one from the other? Perhaps unwittingly, or perhaps because of misunderstandings, the Sioux granted the development of what became three three-mile-wide rights-of-way, which began on the western bank of the Missouri River and crossed their land. Although the treaty denied the

United States entry into the Black Hills themselves, the three roads came "near" the forbidden hills. But where could those who traveled the approved roads from Bismarck, Fort Pierre and Yankton, which was known as the Niobrara Route, go after crossing the Sioux land? It was an impossible situation considering the beckoning and constant crescendo of gold.

Because of these many impasses related to the treaty, along with the disaster Custer and his men suffered at the Little Bighorn River in June 1876 and incidences of violence, the doors to the hills were finally and officially flung open on February 18, 1877. Legislators threw up their hands and approved the Manypenny Act. George Manypenny, who had served as the director of Indian Affairs from 1853 to 1857, was appointed in 1876 to head a special commission to study the situation in the Black Hills. His commission announced to Sioux leaders that, under the agreement of 1877, the Sioux would relinquish their rights to the Black Hills and other lands west of the 103rd meridian. The commission also stated that the Sioux would relinquish their rights to hunt in the unceded territories to the north in exchange for subsistence rations on a permanent reservation for as long as they needed to ensure the survival of the Sioux. It was a take-it-or-leave-it deal. The Sioux called it the "Surrender or Starve Act." Many starved. Few surrendered.

Even before the Manypenny Act, the movement of equipment and supplies to support the mines and thousands of miners and other settlers was well underway into the Black Hills. For the trespassers, the location of the Black Hills in the very center of the Sioux Nation meant they had a long and arduous journey to get to their endowed sanctum. The starting points of the settlers' journeys, including the three legal eastern roads that were approved in the Laramie Treaty, were located at the four compass points surrounding the Black Hills. The other trails were associated with the parallel continental railroads hundreds of miles to the north and south of the hills. Many gold-seekers started their trek from those transcontinental railroads. Others preferred the speed and convenience of taking the train from Sioux City to Yankton and catching a riverboat on the Missouri River to Fort Pierre before heading west on the overland route to Deadwood. Many of these "pilgrims," as the new arrivals to the hills were called, faced a two-hundred-mile journey over the treaty-approved right-of-way that became the famous Fort Pierre to Deadwood Wagon Trail.

It was by far the shortest route to the Black Hills for the thousands of people, and millions of tons of supplies would soon be pulled by bull train over that challenging, dangerous and deadly road. The road, which was laced with gumbo (sticky mud), became a conveyor belt on wooden wagon

Gold miners at work on their claim in a jumbled and dirty street in Deadwood in 1876. *Louis Wendt collection.*

wheels that helped keep the Black Hills alive and productive for a decade. By yoking oxen to work in concert with fast horses and muscular mules, settlers were able to carry all the supplies they needed to mine gold and live on the frontier. The bull trains of oxen that plodded over the Fort Pierre to Deadwood Trail did most of the hard work, hauling hundreds of millions of tons of freight, until the railroad finally punched its way into the hills at Buffalo Gap on the southern slope.

2

THE ROAD

The routes referred to by General Sheridan are three in number—one from Bismarck, one from Fort Pierre and one from Yankton via the Niobrara River. The two routes from Bismarck and Fort Pierre are now being surveyed by order of the territorial authorities, and the government will probably accept the report of that survey and adopt the roads as mounded by the territorial parties. The Niobrara route is still subject to surveying operations, and military officials will soon arrive, whose duty it will be to locate it.

—Press and Dakotian, *Yankton, Dakota Territory, April 4, 1877*

The Fort Pierre to Deadwood Trail was not only the shortest road to the Black Hills but also considered to be the most wagon-friendly route to the gold fields. For the bull team freighters, time was money, and a fast journey over the road west from Fort Pierre meant more cash in the bank. A bull team traversing that two-hundred-mile-long, three-mile-wide road could, in good times, make the trip out and back in a month, and they would retrace their steps, back and forth, at least five or six times a year if the weather was good. As the inevitable snow season approached, the oxen were put out to pasture and relieved from service between the first snowfall of the year and May, when the road would be dried out and ready for more wheels. By charging a fee of three to four cents per pound for hauling, freighters were rewarded handsomely—probably much better than the miners the freighters were serving.

All wasn't milk and honey on that long, hard pull from Fort Pierre to Deadwood. Out on the trail, the bull train's ungulates met up with an occasional steep hill or eroded ravine, and they would sometimes have to plow through a smattering of muddy buffalo wallows and streams. But when the skill of the wagon masters and bullwhackers and the strength of the muscled bulls and sturdy freight wagons combined, the teams would always make it through. Geographic, weather and human barriers may have slowed them down, but the freight haulers never completely stopped; the isolated frontier Black Hills towns required their shipments in order to be productive and to survive.

The most difficult challenge on the trek wasn't the road agent or the stealthy bands of Native Americans who were in quest of contraband—the killers, rustlers and thieves were surely out on the trail waiting among the yuccas and prickly pears in the coulees and canyons—but the Cheyenne River. It was always a part of the long journey, waiting more than one hundred hardscrabble miles out from the Fort Pierre starting point. The Cheyenne River break and the unpredictable waters that had carved it eons ago were among the most difficult challenges for the bull trains. On the edge of the river's steep, rolling break was where the wagon bosses and bullwhackers halted briefly to rest the cattle, sit down on their wagon's shady side and determine the best way to descend the break into the beautiful Cheyenne River Valley. There were many ways to get through the break, but on almost every trip, the odds were that erosion, weather and soil conditions had changed the patterns of the break. The river break, gullies and the final descent prompted wary teamsters to re-check the wagon rough locks and other devices designed to assist in the dicey downhill adventures led by hip-swaying oxen chained to tons of cargo that was stashed carefully in freight wagons trundling behind them. Once the teams were safely on the valley floor, the next challenge was fording the Cheyenne River. The Cheyenne was nothing to be taken for granted; it was the second-largest tributary of the Upper Missouri River. It could run whitewater fast or creep along at an oxen pace east toward the Missouri River depending on the weather upstream.

Once, freighter Charley Zabel decided to give his bulls some relief from a cloud of determined buffalo gnats that was harassing them, so he stopped the bulls in the center of the stream. Zabel later noticed a gradual rise in the river that was caused by heavy rains that were out of sight upstream. Getting the bulls and wagons safely to the shore was a difficult task, he recalled in an August 1933 issue of *Outdoor Life* magazine. The river's banks were steep

After a long journey of two hundred miles from Fort Pierre across the Dakota prairie, bull trains pull into the foothills of the Black Hills, which can be seen in the distance. *South Dakota State Archives.*

and ensnared in brush and high weeds except in the places where other bull teams had eased into the water; however, that activity had also chewed up the mud. To ease the bull train's load, Zabel unhitched the wagons from one another and pulled them across the river one at a time. Fording one wagon at a time made sense and was standard procedure for every freight outfit. After crossing the river and climbing out of the valley, there was no guarantee of safe journey for the remaining eighty miles to the hills. In fact, the closer teams got to the hills, the higher their chances of running into roving bands of bandits or Oceti Sakowin (Sioux) waiting in ambush.

Despite all its difficulties and other travails, the Fort Pierre to Deadwood Trail was hands down the most popular and cost-effective way to travel out of the half dozen trails around the amoeba-shaped Black Hills that sprout, almost magically, out of the prairie in the southwestern corner of the Dakota Territory. The Fort Pierre to Deadwood trail was so well surveyed, traveled and scouted that, a century later, the trail almost matches the route of today's Highway 14. The modern highway crosses over the still-visible 1880 freight wagon wheel ruts and runnels incised in

South Dakota's prairie land twelve times. About forty years ago, the trail and its historic locations were marked by amateur historian Roy Norman of Hayes, South Dakota. Along with his wife, Edith, and at their own expense, Norman made and erected fifty-two signs marking the trail and its memorable stops.

Long before the Normans were able to place their markers, the trail was marked with a sequence of dirt and stone mounds that guided the way. The trail coursed through the vast Sioux lands that had been bound in the 1868 Laramie Treaty. The treaty included a provision for the right-of-way and safe passage of settlers from three points that start on the western shore of the Missouri River. One road that was reserved for trail use, as indicated in the April 4, 1877 edition of the *Press and Dakotian*, was the lengthy 245-mile trek that commenced at Bismarck; another reserved road coursed 200 miles west from Fort Pierre to Deadwood; and a third reserved road wound down the Missouri River at Yankton and was the longest road of

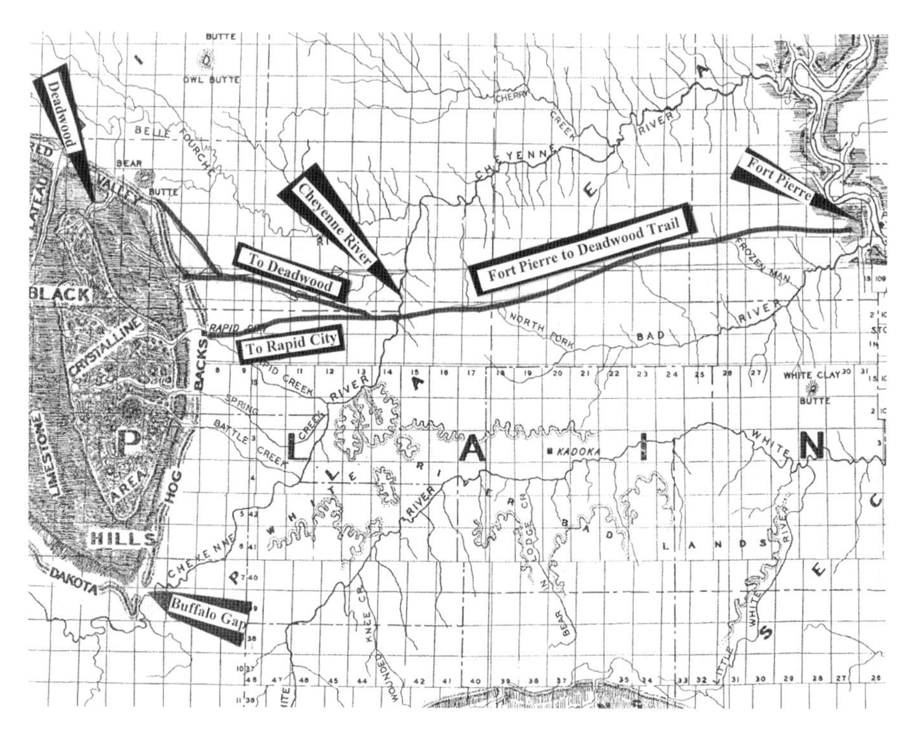

The general route of the Fort Pierre to Deadwood Trail is illustrated in this rendering of the Southwestern Dakota Territory, which is now Western South Dakota. The Missouri River is on the right of the illustration, and the Black Hills are on the far left. *Chuck Cecil collection.*

This sign was made and placed by Roy and Edith Norman on the banks of the Missouri River in Fort Pierre. It marks the beginning of the Fort Pierre to Deadwood Trail. *Lonis Wendt collection.*

the three. As the difficulties of the Yankton Road became apparent—long distance and rough terrain—those looking to reach the hills from Yankton found it easier to follow the western shore of the Missouri River north to Fort Pierre and then head west to the hills from there. Others boarded a riverboat bound for upriver stops. A fourth trail that traveled west from Chamberlain to the Missouri River was later formed on land leased from the Sioux for future use by the Milwaukee Railroad. The right-of-way for this trail was just two hundred yards wide and started on the west bank of the Missouri River. The Milwaukee Railroad paid the Sioux $22,000 or $110 a mile for that trail, according to the April 26, 1879 edition of the *Black Hills Weekly Journal*. The Chamberlain Road was short-lived, however, and soon lost favor with freighters who tried it and returned to traveling along the Fort Pierre to Deadwood Trail. Of course, this all changed when the Northwestern Railroad reached Pierre in 1880; the railroad further established the superiority of the Fort Pierre to Deadwood Trail as the best route to the Black Hills. Those supposedly safe prairie lanes proved to be generous concessions by the Sioux, although experience taught travelers that there was no guarantee of safe passage. But the crude road from Fort Pierre had good grass and water and reduced the travel time to the hills by several days.

The bull trains that were bound for the Black Hills were following the Fort Pierre to Deadwood Trail that had been reconnoitered and mapped in 1855 by famed army cartographer, Lieutenant G.K. Warren. He described the route as "barren with some plateaus covered with grass," according to Delwin Jensen's *Fort Pierre Trail*. Warren's trail was seldom used until Custer's gold discoveries in 1874. Three years later, Deputy U.S. Surveyor Edward Palmer was sent out to scout the trail again, adjust it as necessary and throw up dirt mounds as guides. He estimated one could travel the road to the hills "with ease" in five days with a good team of horses. His estimates would change. The *Black Hills Daily Times* reported that as stagecoach lines were improved on, the trip from Fort Pierre to Deadwood by stage was shortened to about thirty-five hours.

In 1877, the newly organized Evans and Hornick Freight Company recognized the advantages of the Fort Pierre to Deadwood Trail. The *Black Hills Daily Times* reported in its July 17, 1879 edition that the company was soon unloading three Sioux City–based riverboats a day at its four Fort Pierre warehouses, where goods awaited transfer by bull trains for the western trek, in order to respond to the number of orders that were being placed for goods in the hills. From then on, nearly all that was needed to dig out gold

In this early sketch of the Fred T. Evans Freight Line warehouse at Fort Pierre, a steamer filled with goods that had been ordered by Black Hills merchants in Deadwood is unloaded as bullwhackers line up to be loaded for the two-hundred-mile journey overland to the Black Hills. *South Dakota State Archives.*

and survive on the frontier's fringe was carried on the three conveyances of that day: railroads, riverboats and freight wagons drawn by oxen, mules and horses for the final two-hundred-mile leg. A vast array of supplies was sent upriver on steamboats from Sioux City and Yankton to Fort Pierre, where it was briefly stored in the Evans and Hornick warehouses or others that were owned by Downer T. Bramble of Yankton, the Northwest Express, Stage and Freight Company and other operators on the Missouri River's western shore to await its bull train assignment.

Hornick soon left his partnership with Evans, which was when Evans began to organize what became the largest and most successful freighting outfit on the trail. Evans was well known, trusted and admired. He had experience on the trails to the Black Hills before anyone else, and he knew the bull train transportation business better than anyone. By 1877, he was dispatching ten to forty tons of goods a day, seven days a week, on the Fort Pierre to Deadwood Trail. His hundreds of bull trains would each make five or six trips to the Black Hills each year, packing in more than a million pounds of freight for an average charge of two to five cents per pound, according to the June 7, 1877 edition of the *Black Hills Daily Times*.

Freight wagons powered by oxen, mules and occasionally horses all departed from Fort Pierre near what is known today as the terminus of Hustan Avenue, near the southwest end of the Waldron Missouri River Bridge. After their departure, the bull trains would turn west to slowly climb up out of the narrow Missouri River Basin; the climb to the high plains was a tough eleven-mile pull. Upon reaching the crest—depending on the time of day the wagons had moved out from Fort Pierre—the bull train wagon boss might order everyone to camp for the night at Willow Creek. If the train had started early in the day or if they had good weather and lively bulls, the wagons may have been allowed to reach Ash Creek and plug on for a few more miles to the aptly named Lance Creek, which is about twenty-five miles west of Fort Pierre. There are two versions of the story about how Lance Creek was named, according to Virginia Driving Hawk Sneve's book *Geographic Place Names*. One version claims a native's knife was found along the creek's bank. The other version says that a surgeon's lance was found along the little stream.

Once the bull trains were back on the trail shortly after sunup the next day, they would rattle on for several miles before crossing what became known as Frozenman's Creek, which is in what is now known as South Dakota's Stanley County. The creek was named after two soldiers and a Sioux warrior were found dead along the creek during a cold Dakota

Landmark Grindstone Butte, which is around the halfway mark of the Fort Pierre to Deadwood Trail. *Lonis Wendt collection.*

winter. On May 6, 1884, the *Black Hills Daily Times* reported that a stabbing incident had occurred at the Frozenman's Creek crossing. A night-herder and the boss of a bull train that was owned by a man named Hart were arguing; during the discussion, the wagon boss was "dangerously stabbed" and taken back to Fort Pierre for treatment.

Near the modern-day, watch fob–sized community of Hayes, South Dakota, is Highway 14, which follows the old path of the bull trains that headed southwest over the prairie's vast expanse, lumbered over desolate country and forded Plum Creek near the Stanley and Haakon County line. Sticky soil called gumbo could often be found on the trail to Deadwood; the soil was benign in dry weather, but after it rained, it became nasty, clinging mud that men, bulls and wagons had to contend with. The wagons slogged through the gumbo toward the pristine prairie country in the Grindstone Butte area. The Cheyenne River Valley could be seen in the distance as the slow-rolling, white-bonneted armadas threaded their way between stately Grindstone Butte and the smaller buttes on the sage-strewn prairie.

As the traffic of bull trains and pioneer homesteaders on the trail to Deadwood increased, a roadhouse was constructed from flat grindstone slabs that had been sloughed off Grindstone Butte centuries earlier. The *Rapid City Journal* reported that the roadhouse was transformed into a telegraph station for the Rapid City, Fort Meade and Missouri telegraph line in early 1938. The *Journal* later reported:

> *When the telegraph line was burned by Indians, who set fire to the prairie between the White River and the Cheyenne River in 1892 in an effort to keep cattle from the country, it was decided the station was no longer needed, and the line was never rebuilt. It was outside the door of the old station that the agent, Mexican Ed, was shot by "Alligator" Allen after an argument over cards. The agent's body was found the next morning by cowboys Tom O'Brien and John Q. Peterson, who covered the body with a wagon box to protect it while they rode to Fort Pierre to get the coroner.*

Many of the old building's grindstone slabs were removed years later and used in the construction of a cattle barn.

Farther west from Grindstone Butte was the Cheyenne River Valley. The valley could be a haven or a hazard for travelers, depending on the weather. In good weather, the valley was lush with grass for the ox teams and provided wood for the teamsters' campfires, and in harsh winter storms, the valley provided shelter from the stinging prairie winds. If bull trains encountered bad weather in the Grindstone Butte area, their goal was to reach the Cheyenne Valley as quickly as possible and hunker down there to wait out the storm.

The blizzards that occurred in early January 1880 were particularly hard on the bull trains. Some freighters gambled on the weather holding, but they lost the bet. Hundreds of cattle died on the trail that year. They were worn down and in miserable condition, unable to find grass in the deep snow. The Cheyenne River Valley became crowded with freight wagons. The *Black Hills Daily Times* in Deadwood reported, "Some [freighters] have gone into winter quarters owing to the loss of cattle." Bullwhackers stripped trees of bark and twigs to feed their cattle on the trail. Charley Zabel, whose bull trains were stranded in the valley that year, told *Outdoor Life* magazine that deer and antelope in the valley suffered even more than the longhorns from sunny, warm Texas. He recalled seeing deer and antelope weak and stranded in deep snow banks. Teamsters roped the animals for slaughter and consumed their much-needed meat.

The *Black Hills Daily Times* reported that a Waldron and Shaffer bull train was one among a group that was stranded in the valley for nearly five weeks. Bullwhacker Bob Herkin was also stuck in the snow during the storm and lost thirty oxen. Outfits belonging to Charley Dyer and Foley and McHume also pulled up and wintered in the valley. Every living thing suffered; the snow in the valley was more than a foot deep and continued to fall. To

The remains of the old Grindstone post office and stage station in Western Haakon County, South Dakota. The station was named after the nearby Grindstone Butte. The foundation stones in this picture are grindstones that were removed from an outcropping of the coarse sandstone on that butte. *Lonis Wendt collection.*

clear away the snow, freighters chopped trees, tied them to yokes of oxen and circled a wide area; this cleared enough snow for the cattle to find a smattering of wilted grasses. The following year, the *Black Hills Daily Times* reported that a freighter named Ingersoll was also stranded in the Cheyenne River Valley by a series of blizzards that most likely began in November. He finally made it to Deadwood—which is one hundred miles away from the valley—on April 7, 1881.

While the winter blizzards caused delays and suffering for the bull trains, the summer droughts that were interspersed with heavy rains also slowed and halted the rolling conveyor belt of freight wagons across the plains. In the July 23, 1880 issue of the *Black Hills Daily Times*, readers learned of a heavy rainfall that was causing delays.

> *Frank Whitney, the boss on a freighter on the Pierre route, came in Wednesday last and delivered for the Evans line 150,000 pounds of freight. From him, we learned that the prospects are not very flattering for the next five weeks. During the early part of the season, it was so dry that the grass attained no height and had become so dry that it would burn, until about a month ago when it turned in and rained nearly all the time. An*

Smithville Crossing on the Cheyenne River. *Lonis Wendt collection.*

> *immense amount of water fell, more than has ever been known to fall before in the same length of time.*
>
> *Streams that usually have but little water in them were from six to ten feet deep, and ravines that were not worthy of the name of creeks were axle deep to the wagon for weeks. And when it comes to talk about mud, they have it down there* [on the prairie] *and so deep that it is almost impassable. For the next three weeks, he says there will be no bull trains* [coming] *in that do not come in within a day or two. He says that men are scouring the country in every direction between the Cheyenne crossing and Pierre looking for grass to make hay of, but there is none to speak of anywhere near the road.*

The *Deadwood Press* reported: "Freighters on the Pierre route express great fears of a general famine along the line as far as cattle are concerned." The *Black Hills Weekly Journal* in Rapid City agreed. "The many freight routes in and out of the hills to the various railroads are known by the carcasses of many a hard-worked ox and horse with which the public roads are lined from one year's end to another. Hundreds and even thousands are thus sacrificed every season."

All along the road from Fort Pierre to the Cheyenne River, the soil was particularly bothersome with clinging mud called gumbo. When the gumbo was wet, it would mix with the dead grasses of the prairie and become a clinging mass that would stick to the cattle's cloven hooves and bullwhackers' worn boots. The gumbo stuck like glue to the wagons' wheels and gathered layer after layer with every turn. Eventually, the layers of mud packed

In wet weather, gumbo mud and dried prairie grasses were the scourge of the Fort Pierre to Deadwood freight wagons. The sticky mud collected in great masses on the wagon wheels, the oxen's hooves and the boots of the bullwhackers. *Photo by Sissy Snyderman.*

between the wheels and wagon boxes acted like brakes, and the added weight of the mud to wheels, boots and hooves often brought caravans to a halt. In its April 26, 1879 issue, the *Black Hills Weekly Journal* at Rapid City reported on the formidable challenges the gumbo caused.

> *Freighters and stages on the Black Hills routes are just now in a desperate struggle with gumbo, which means mud in bottomless deposits, mud that takes hold like a lightning rod peddler and is hard to shake off. But it is consoling to know it does not take the winds and warm sunshine long to dry up muddy roads in this country.*

On June 10, 1881, the *Black Hills Daily Times* reported, "Rain showers along the line of the Fort Pierre route have been copious during the past ten days, softening the track to such an extent as to render the progress of heavy freight trains, if not impossible, at least impracticable, and they are all resting in camp, awaiting the stiffening of the gumbo."

Oxen that were pulling particularly heavy loads over the prairie didn't always travel the desired fifteen miles a day. In May 1882, the *Black Hills Daily Times* reported that a bull team slogged its way through the gumbo mud on the Fort Pierre to Deadwood Trail for thirty-four days, which means they traveled at an average speed of just six miserable miles a day. A year later, in July 1883, news appeared in the *Daily Times* of a man named Evans arriving with his bull trains on July 5 after a sixty-day journey. When teams encountered gumbo, it was usually necessary to unhook the three wagons and pull each separately through the quagmire.

In 1881, the Missouri River flooded the Fort Pierre area, damaging and destroying the community. The loading docks in the freight storage area, the derricks, a number of bulls and hundreds of thousands of dollars' worth of goods and merchandise awaiting transport to the hills were destroyed and taken down the swollen river, according to the *South Dakota Historical Society Quarterly*.

As the Fort Pierre to Deadwood Trail became more popular for stagecoach travel, relay stations were established every twelve miles at places like Willow Creek, Ottumwa, Medicine Creek, Grindstone, the Bad River, Peno Springs, Deadman's Creek and the Hole. The Hole was a watering spot about ten miles north of what would become known as the town of Wicksville on Highway 14. In Jan Cerney's *The Fort Pierre-Deadwood Gold Trail*, she describes the crude houses and barns that were built for humans and horses at the relay stations. Hay and grain for the stagecoach horses was stored at these relay stations, and wells were dug at many of the stations that were far from water.

As the bull trains neared the Black Hills, an exit near Washta Springs veered off the main trail and led to the growing community of Rapid City. Rapid City's strategic location at a natural gateway into the hills transformed the small camp—where men once harvested hay—into the most prominent city in the Black Hills, much to the chagrin of Deadwood promoters. During the gold rush days, Deadwood considered itself the main community and distribution center of the Black Hills, but Rapid City eventually took those bragging rights when the railroad rolled into town, ignoring Deadwood as it coursed along the eastern and northern edges of the hills. But until the railroads arrived in Buffalo Gap in 1885, the conveyor belt of wagons kept to its task of delivering supplies to the southern reaches of the Black Hills. The arrival of the railroad was the beginning of the end of the bull trains, but for a dozen years or so, the hoof-friendly Fort Pierre to Deadwood Trail was, without a doubt, the Dakota Territory's busiest superhighway and a godsend to the people and industries of the Black Hills.

3

THE FREIGHT

If all the teams employed by Dougherty and Company in freighting from Pierre to the Black Hills should arrive at the same time, they would unload the immense amount of 1,174,500 pounds.

—Pierre Signal, *Pierre, Dakota Territory, August 1, 1880*

Bull trains were numerous yesterday and will continue to arrive every day, as we hear that the road is lined with them from here to Pierre, interspersed with many families of emigrants.

—Black Hills Daily Times, *Deadwood, Dakota Territory, October 18, 1883*

Overland freighters were quick to envision the potential of teaming up for long-haul treks into the hills. They took particular note of the plight of the Black Hills miners that were already digging in the forbidden Paha Sapa. In a letter home to Yankton from Deadwood, which was published in the October 27, 1876 issue of the *Black Hills Daily Times*, G.W. Newton, one of the earliest Black Hills miners, mentioned the miners' critical need for supplies. "We are all well, fat and dirty," he wrote. "There will be a party leaving here tomorrow for Fort Pierre to get [wagons] in with provisions. A [wagon] loaded with provisions could get any price they would ask."

Despite the lack of supplies in the Black Hills, miners were so intent on traveling to the area that they were willing to pay any price. In June 1877, one determined and creative soul left Cheyenne, in the Wyoming Territory, on foot, pushing a wheelbarrow. His final destination of Deadwood was 292 miles away. Tied firmly in his wheelbarrow were his basic travel needs: bedding, food, a pot and a pan, a shovel and a pickaxe. This unusual trip was confirmed by G.W. Newton and H.L. McIvaine. In the June 15, 1877 edition of the *Black Hills Daily Times*, the men reported that they had seen the man and his wheelbarrow when they passed him in their Deadwood-bound stagecoach. However, when their stagecoach and sweat-lathered horses jangled into Deadwood fourteen days later, they were told that the wheelbarrow man had arrived the previous day.

On October 23, 1883, the *Pierre Signal* told of a party of Black Hills miners who had just arrived in Pierre from Deadwood with gold-laden pockets. "One man had five pounds of it, and all were planning to return to the hills after they had re-supplied. They were offering $10 a day for workmen to accompany them." Today, this offer for workmen would amount to around $200 per day. One of Deadwood's newspapers wrote about a man who found a "$21 nugget in the roots of a beet he had dug up in his backyard."

Some miners who made the long journey soon gave up the hunt for gold. One man headed east on foot after mining in the hills with no results; he hoped to homestead on a farm in Bon Homme County, near Springfield in the Southeastern Dakota Territory. In 1883, the *Pierre Signal* reported that the man's walk of two hundred miles, from Deadwood to Fort Pierre, took him just five days. The speedy walker wasn't the only disappointed gold-seeker to give up his quest for riches and leave the hills. Many miners left, trailing along behind plodding bull trains that were headed back to Fort Pierre for another load of supplies. Others rode their horses or took a stagecoach back to what everyone in Deadwood referred to as "civilization." Thousands left the hills with empty pockets; many of them were already poverty-stricken when they arrived, and they left with pockets that were even more threadbare.

In 1877, a Deadwood editor mockingly observed, "One hundred passengers left Deadwood today. They could not see any gold on the sidewalk. Deadwood can very well spare this class of people, for no one ever attained success without earnest effort." Despite this high rate of failure, migrants kept pouring into the hills. A popular four-line poem from the early years in the Black Hills contains humor and truth:

No coats on their backs,
No pockets for bills,
But still they are flocking,
To the dreary Black Hills.

A steady line of gold-seekers could be found in every train station back east in "civilization," and they were each intending to test their mettle in the gold mines of the Black Hills. This fact was evident from a series of travel news items in the March and April 1877, issues of the *Yankton Press and Dakotian*. A March 17 story from the newspaper reported, "A party of Black Hillers [another name for Black Hills migrants] from Austin, Minnesota, arrived in Yankton today. The boys were fourteen days on the road and experienced some rough weather, but the teams are looking well. These gentlemen will leave for the hills in a few days after resting their teams and laying in new supplies." On March 24, the newspaper reported, "A party of one hundred men are expected to leave Chicago on the third of April for the hills via Yankton and the Missouri River to Fort Pierre." The same issue also reported, "One hundred Black Hillers have received passage for Pierre on Burleigh's boats to start as soon as ice is out of the river." On April 6, the newspaper reported: "Four hundred men arrived on last night's train from Sioux City, mostly for the Black Hills. It took four coaches to bring them."

A determined turkey farmer from Elk Point, located in the far southeastern corner of the Dakota Territory, started his journey to Deadwood in 1879 with a raft of 350 turkeys. His gobbling "herd" did just fine until after they were ferried across the Missouri River from Pierre to Fort Pierre. Once the turkeys were at last on the vast prairie, their flashing, bright-red wattles caught the sharp, searching eyes and sensitive noses of the area's wolves and coyotes. By the time the farmer and his skittish flock reached the hills, their numbers had shrunk to just thirty-two birds. The turkey herder joked at his journey's end that he wasn't that concerned about the loss of turkeys; he jokingly told a reporter from the *Yankton Press and Dakotian* that he only took them along to give him something to do on his trip to the gold fields.

The feverish human tide to the Black Hills continued, unfettered, into the 1870s. They pushed wheelbarrows, minded turkeys, bullwhacked wagons, skinned mules, rode horses, hiked and rode riverboats to get there. The wealthy entrepreneurs who intended to buy mines and banks lit up their Marksman and White Owl cigars as they rocked west in stagecoaches.

Deadwood, the destination of most who were bound for the hills, was a noisy, muddy place that was teeming with life. The first need of all new arrivals was shelter, so trees had to be felled and lumber had to be sawn into planks by hand. The sawyers in Deadwood, however, couldn't keep up with the demand, so sawmills were disassembled back east and freighted by bull teams to Deadwood. "Brauch and Wood have gotten their mill into the hills

Deadwood's busy—and muddy—main street around 1876. *South Dakota State Historical Society's Morrow collection.*

at last," reported the *Yankton Press and Dakotian* on August 10, 1876. "It is now lying at Camp Crook on Rapid Creek. If they do not set it up within the next couple of years, they may have some trouble in finding any timber to saw," the story concluded, referring to the deforestation in the hills around the appropriately named Deadwood. For a time, freighters also hauled flour to Deadwood that sold for small fortunes. When writing to friends in Yankton in the Eastern Dakota Territory, J.W. Owens, a miner, told of a gold-seeker who offered him one hundred dollars in gold for a sack of flour. "There is plenty of gold and a great scarcity of grub in the hills," he wrote in his letter, which was published on May 23, 1876, in the *Yankton Press and Dakotian*. Eastern flourmills were dismantled or made and loaded on riverboats for the upstream paddle to Fort Pierre. After 1880, when the Northwestern Railroad reached Pierre, the mills arrived by rail.

At the peak of the gold rush, the number of mines in the hills grew to around three hundred. All of them needed stamp mills and a plethora of other heavy equipment, including rails for horizontal mine tunnels and lifts for mine shafts, in order to operate. In August 1881, the Homestake Mine ordered 150 tons of steel rail, and according to the October 27, 1881 issue of the *Black Hills Daily Times*, it was hauled to the hills by bull trains. Miles of cabling and piping were also delivered to the mine from Fort Pierre aboard the lumbering freight wagons. In November 1879, the Fred Evans Transportation Company's bull trains pulled through Deadwood and on to Lead City to deliver a monstrous 23,000-pound iron wheel for a mine's hoisting works. As described in the *Black Hills Daily Times*, the wheel was divided into two parts, and each half of the wheel was carefully hoisted by block and tackle pulleys aboard two freight wagons at Evans's warehouse in Fort Pierre. The two "truck wagons," each with a capacity of ten tons, were pulled across the plains from Fort Pierre by two teams of twenty slobbering oxen. With heavy loads such as this, freighters would haul in the hot months, when the trail was dry and hard.

The mines also needed tons of dynamite—known to miners as Giant Powder after its manufacturer's name—in order to reach their caches. In 1882, the *Black Hills Daily Times* reported that wagons, men and oxen from the Fred Evans Company unloaded and stored 150,000 pounds of Giant

The huge Homestake Mine in Lead, near Deadwood, in 1950. The mine, which is North America's deepest and largest, was opened in the late 1870s and continued to produce gold until 2002. While it was operating, the mine yielded nearly forty-four million troy ounces of gold. A portion of the mine is now dedicated to the National Science Foundation's Deep Underground Science and Engineering Laboratory. *Chuck Cecil collection.*

Powder in Homestake Mine's magazines. Another lot of 25,000 pounds awaited the wagon caravan's return to Fort Pierre for another two-hundred-mile trek to the mine. Even after the railroad finally reached the Black Hills in 1884, shipments of blasting powder for the mines continued to be delivered by bull teams out of Fort Pierre. The railroads' rates for hauling explosives was extremely high, so using the bull trains for this task was the cheapest option. In 1877, according to Deadwood's *Black Hills Daily Times*, 150 tons of powder was lugged by oxen over the Fort Pierre to Deadwood Trail. In 1885, even after the railroad had reached the hills, one lonely bull train was still plodding over the Fort Pierre to Deadwood Trail, pulling wagons loaded with 300,000 pounds of dynamite to the mines. While there were always prairie fires started by campfires, lightning, bullwhackers' lighted pipes and sparks from iron wheels to worry about, there were no explosions caused by Giant Powder on the Fort Pierre to Deadwood Trail.

More worrisome, however, was the danger of Giant Powder accidentally erupting in the City of Deadwood as the wagons trundled through to nearby Lead City and the mines. In August 1885, the *Black Hills Daily Times* editorialized:

> *The wonder is that with vast quantities of explosives constantly in transit to and through the city, accidents, including fatalities, are not almost an everyday occurrence. Yesterday, a* Times *reporter peered into an unloading freight wagon and beheld a box of Giant Powder, several of which were broken* [with] *cartridges falling out. The cargo had been transported over two hundred miles from Pierre over a road* [that was] *at no time in the best condition. Teamsters handle such freight seemingly with no greater thought or care than they do the most harmless freight, and yet, sufficient concussion would explode an entire load, sending a large portion of the city to kingdom come.*

Fortunately, there was no blasting powder aboard a freight wagon on the Fort Pierre Trail in February 1883. A night-herder named Polo Bernard drank too much on his night patrol and fell asleep in a wagon with a lighted pipe in his mouth. The pipe set fire to his bedding, and Bernard was badly burned. The *Pierre Signal* reported that he later died from his injuries.

In the late 1800s, the accumulating masses of men, women and children in the isolated hills were in need of all the goods that supported life on the plains. Nearly all of it had to be hauled in, mostly by oxen, although mule teams and horses did their share of the hard work. Some of what was needed in the hills could be provided locally, including meat and potatoes, salt from nearby salt flats, clay bricks and garden produce. But the vast majority of goods needed in the hills was shipped in freight wagons. In June 1880, Hermann and Treber's Saloon received what the *Black Hills Daily Times* described as "the largest invoice of St. Louis beer that ever came to a firm in this city in one day." The newspaper editor humorously added, "There were 200 barrels containing, in all, 14,400 quart bottles of the beverage that cheers but never intoxicates."

Fuel for lamps and stoves was a highly demanded commodity in the hills. There was plenty of firewood, but coal and fuel oil had to be muscled in by bulls over the Fort Pierre to Deadwood Trail. During particularly cold winters, when the oil supply dwindled beyond expectations, emergency trips had to be made. Mason Martin of Pierre made one emergency trip from Fort Pierre in December 1880. His bull train carried two tons of kerosene that had been ordered by a Deadwood dealer. Martin recounted his 1880 trip in the Hughes County History pamphlet published by the county superintendent of schools in February 1937. In the pamphlet, Martin said

Postcard of an original photograph of a busy Deadwood street during the gold rush of the 1870s and 1880s. Note the sign hanging under the pocket watch replica on the left side of the photograph that is inscribed with "Herrmann and Treber." In June 1880, the *Black Hills Daily Times* in Deadwood reported that Herrmann and Treber had received the largest-ever Black Hills shipment of St. Louis beer. The two-hundred-barrel shipment was delivered from Fort Pierre by bull train. *Chuck Cecil collection.*

that when his wagons reached the Cheyenne River, about one hundred miles west of Pierre, he was met by an emissary that had been sent out by the Deadwood dealer to meet him and urge him to hurry along. Martin said the man mentioned Deadwood's dire needs and offered him a fifty-dollar bonus if the bull train got to Deadwood by a proposed date. By pushing his team, Martin met the deadline. The customers in Deadwood were so desperate for the fuel that they did not wait for it to be unloaded. The cans of fuel were sold directly out of the wagons at two dollars per gallon, which was twice the cost in Fort Pierre. Despite the high price, the fuel was gone in two minutes.

Freighters on the wagon road had many stipulations on freighting rates and requirements, including how their freight should be packaged for wagon shipment. Rates were applied in one-hundred-pound increments with no exceptions; if a customer ordered fifty pounds of goods, or any weight below one hundred pounds, the rate was still based on the one-hundred-pound increment. Freighters also wanted advance payment or guarantees for the shipment of mining and farm machinery and perishable goods. Freight charges included any riverboat or railroad transportation that was required to get products to Fort Pierre. According to Deadwood newspaper advertisements from 1876 to the early 1880s, the combined charge for one hundred pounds of goods usually ranged from $2.50 to $3.00 per pound. For one hundred pounds of freight, the rate went up to $25.00 or $30.00 per one hundred pounds. Most of that cost went to the railroad and steamship owners; the bull train freighter's share could vary between $0.02 and $0.10 per pound.

The rates over the Fort Pierre to Deadwood Trail were much less than what had to be charged to shippers using the longer, more difficult trails out of Sidney, Nebraska; Cheyenne, Wyoming; and Bismarck and Yankton in the Dakota Territory. According to the June 4, 1876 issue of the *Yankton Press and Dakotian*, freighters hauling from Custer to Deadwood in the Black Hills, a distance of just seventy-five miles, charged seven cents per pound. Comparatively, Dick Dunn, a freighter on the road from Fort Pierre to Deadwood, charged just three cents per pound. Freighters on the Cheyenne route acknowledged in late 1876 that they could not transport freight in competition with Fort Pierre rates, according to a report from the *Press and Dakotian*. The price discrepancy was so pronounced that it wasn't long before many Nebraska, Wyoming, Bismarck and Yankton freighters moved most of their outfits to Fort Pierre so they could compete for business.

In July 1880, Graves and Barney built a three-story brick building in Deadwood. Bull trains delivered the heavy decorative iron for the building's façade, and the freight charge from Fort Pierre to the hills for these heavier transports was more expensive than usual fare. For example, the Fred Evans Transportation Company hauled machinery for the Cross Gold Mining Company for eight cents per pound, or eight dollars per one hundred pounds, according to a January 1884 newspaper advertisement in the *Black Hills Daily Times*.

Bull trains were the least expensive option for shipping due to the lower purchase and maintenance costs of oxen compared to mules and horses; oxen were less expensive and didn't need harnesses or iron shoes. However, because of what was being shipped, some freight rates had an add-on price of half or double the published rate due to the possibility of moisture damage, spoilage or other damage on the jarring wagon ride. This addition was included with the shipment of items like dry goods, clothing, printing press paper, carpets (except oil cloth), boots and shoes packed in cases, glassware in casks, crockery in casks and crates, organs, pianos, eggs in barrels and cases, and interestingly, green apples and empty beer kegs. Double rate charges were levied for the shipment of such things as mirrors, sewing machines ("unless knocked down and boxed"), carriages, burial cases (caskets), boxed toys, sleds and toy wagons, plus other similar items, according to newspaper advertisements placed by the Northwestern Railroad.

Much of the day-to-day commerce in Deadwood was conducted using gold dust as currency. On the counter of nearly every business was a small scale to calculate the gold exchange. Prices were usually set in even dollar amounts that could be quickly computed. Nothing in Deadwood was sold in odd cents, such as ninety-nine cents or thirty-seven cents. In April 1877, a town meeting of business owners agreed that Deadwood's price of gold dust would be set at twenty dollars per ounce. This would fluctuate with the inflation rate of the time; a year later, the town's merchants met and reduced the price of gold to seventeen dollars per ounce. There was a 10 percent discount if customers paid in greenbacks, according to the April 15, 1950 issue of the *Rapid City Journal*. To protect the gold and keep it from all of the town's saloons, dance halls and stores, the Stebbins, Post and Mudd Bank in Deadwood bought a new 6,400-pound safe that arrived on a specially reinforced freight wagon powered by a ten-yoke bull team on September 29, 1879. The safe's shipment, documented in the *Black Hills Daily Times*, was delayed for more than a week, because its first freight wagon, which was loaded in Fort Pierre, broke down under its weight. A reinforced wagon and a sturdy gin pole with a pulley and ropes were sent out to where the damaged wagon waited, ninety miles west of Fort Pierre.

A crew of strong men muscled the three-ton safe onto the new wagon, and the delivery was safely made.

The thousands of independent gold-seekers who worked the rockers on muddy stream banks or spent their days knee-deep in cold creek water while swirling a placer pan also needed shovels, pickaxes, axes, saws and all that living in a tent required. Venison and buffalo meat was always nearby, but a diet of wild meat did not suffice. John B. Pearson of Yankton, who had been successful on his second attempt to gain entry into the then-forbidden Black Hills, arrived there on May 4, 1875, with six others. Pearson and the others commenced mining in the Whitewood area, and in the June 6, 1876 edition of the *Yankton Press and Dakotian*, Pearson recalled the difficulty of subsisting solely on what he called "jerked deer." Desperate for food variety, Pearson and

Two five-yoke bull teams that are pulling three wagons each pass through an unknown frontier Black Hills town in early winter. The wagons were probably carrying the camping equipment of the men managing the teams. *South Dakota State Archives.*

another member of his party went to Fort Laramie and purchased enough supplies to last six months. The men dodged military patrols and made it back into the hills with their goods loaded on a train of twelve wagons.

Everything a society on the frontier's fringe could need, and much that it didn't, was delivered by bull trains. When the wagons and bulls arrived, they were parked on Deadwood's narrow Main Street, as close to the merchants' front doors as possible. Merchants and their clerks helped unload the wagons and neatly refill Deadwood's depleted store shelves and display cabinets. The efforts of freighters kept food on people's tables and coal in their stoves. Bull trains delivered nails, door latches, small panes of window glass and other accoutrements that were needed to build the crude log cabins and lean-tos that were crowded, cheek by jowl, on the flats and clung precariously to Deadwood's steep canyon walls. On the frontier, clothing eventually wore out and needed mending, so the huge freight wagons also carried boxes of pins, needles, thread, buckles, snaps and buttons that were ordered by Black Hills merchants. In her book *Old Deadwood Days*, Estelline Bennett said that when a customer complained about a twenty-five-cent charge for one small sewing needle, the merchant blamed the high price on the transportation costs he paid to get the needle to his store.

Schools in the hills needed desks, books, chalk, blackboards and bells to beckon the schoolchildren. Churches needed hymnals and baptismal fonts. Everyone needed soap, especially the bullwhackers just arriving from weeks of eating dust. Bathing businesses, which were usually affiliated with barbershops, made nice profits renting out tubs and clean towels and selling hot water. Miners and their families often ordered musical instruments and sheet music to go with them. According to newspaper advertisements from that time, people in the hills would also pay good money and gold dust for bow ties, suspenders, clocks, dancing shoes, roller and ice skates and much more. Medicines and pieces of medical equipment were packed for shipment in sturdy wooden boxes. A profusion of other supplies arrived in barrels. Bull trains brought in farm machinery, blacksmithing equipment, bakery ovens, barber chairs and razor strops, church organs and reams of newsprint for Deadwood's newspapers. All that and much more was lugged over the prairie to the hills, mostly by bull trains.

According to Estelline Bennett's *Old Deadwood Days*, the first piano to tinkle its melodious tunes in the Black Hills was brought by a wagon pulled by twenty oxen from the railhead at Bismarck in 1876. It took the bull team two months of slogging over 250 miles of muddy, rain-drenched trail to get the heavy instrument to Deadwood's popular Bella Union Theater.

In 1877, Deadwood had three churches and seventy-three saloons, which the local editor facetiously called "elegant cocktail exchanges," according to Doane Robinson's book *History of South Dakota*. The owners of those smoky "cocktail exchanges" ordered felt-covered poker tables, hefty beer mugs that were nearly unbreakable during brief barroom scuffles, cards, poker chips and large mirrors to mount behind their shiny, brass-railed bars. The saloon owners also needed Brunswick and Balke pool tables, cue chalk, eight balls, and most importantly, barrels of beer and whiskey that many locals called "bunch." On December 16, 1879, the *Black Hills Daily Times* announced that a bull train loaded with 175 barrels of bunch had rolled into town. Loads of booze never ceased to arrive. In August 1879, bull trains arrived in Deadwood with a load of nineteen-dollar-per-barrel Falk's Milwaukee beer. Each barrel contained seventy-two quarts of beer that was sold at the bar in pint glasses for a quarter; the profits nearly doubled the barrel's wholesale cost.

Eggs were also in great demand in the hills before freighters brought in chickens. Before the hens arrived, eggs were shipped during cooler, above-freezing weather, individually wrapped and buried in barrels of oats for protection. Eggs were priced at ten cents per dozen in Yankton and sold in Deadwood for sixty cents per dozen. In the very early pioneering years, Jim Wardner made a fortune in the egg business. The *Black Hills Daily Times* reported that Wardner would purchase a massive amount of eggs in the Eastern Dakota Territory and Iowa for as little as nine cents per dozen and then sell them for a huge profit in Deadwood. Before apple trees could be planted and nursed along to produce fruit in the hills, apples were also in great demand. During the fall, apples from "civilization" would be wrapped in paper and placed in barrels of grain husks to protect them from freezing during shipment, but the grain husks often didn't protect the apples. If apples froze on the way, they were cooked and squeezed into cider in Deadwood. In October 1876, the *Yankton Press and Dakotian* released a story about an entrepreneur from Yankton that had made his way to Deadwood and set to work digging up seedling Black Hills pine trees. After digging up the seedlings, the man would pack them in dirt and moss and bring them back to Yankton, where they were sold for fifty cents each.

Until it became common for farms and ranches in the hills to keep milk cows, butter was shipped to the West in large quantities during the colder months. Fruits and vegetables were subject to spoilage and often shipped by what was called fast freight on stagecoaches or lighter horse-drawn farm wagons. Wardner, who used his egg profits to buy Deadwood's Red Front Store, was the first merchant to sell oysters in Deadwood and he had them shipped by fast freight. As stagecoach travel agendas and routes were improved and changes in shipping procedures were made, stage companies introduced what they called lightning freight. Sacks of mail, hundreds of pounds at a time, were sent by stagecoach on the Deadwood Trail by lightning freight. The much slower, sure-footed bull trains traveled on or near the same paths as the stagecoaches. They did not always cross paths, however; the trail was a mile or more wide, and stagecoaches and freight wagons would pick the best route depending on road conditions and the availability of grass for the oxen.

The bull trains lugged some unusual things into the hills as well. On August 22, 1882, the *Black Hills Daily Times* reported that a twenty-two-inch narrow-gauge locomotive weighing more than five tons had made the long trip from Fort Pierre to Deadwood, making it the first locomotive in the Black Hills. The wagon boss on that delivery was Robert Flormann, who later bought the Uncle Sam Gold Mine near Nemo. He later sold the mine to eastern interests, and with the profits, he built a handsome three-story brick building in downtown Rapid City. The area on which the building was constructed is still known in Rapid City as the Flormann Block. The engine Flormann bullwhacked to Lead City was named the J.J. Haggin in honor of a successful Homestake Gold Mine investor. Before the very productive Homestake Gold Mine closed in 2002, it was the deepest and largest gold mine in the world. Just two years after Flormann delivered the locomotive, another even larger locomotive was hauled westward by mule teams from Fort Pierre to the mine. The new engine was named after the principal mine owner and billionaire George Hearst of California.

Many other unusual consignments found their way to the hills aboard bull train wagons. Wild Bill Hickok's ornate Italian marble gravestone, ordered by Wild Bill's good friend Colorado Charley, was brought overland on a bull train freight wagon. In November 1883, the *Black Hills Daily Times* reported that a load of live German carp was shipped by the U.S. Fish and Fisheries Commission to a Black Hills customer. The shipment was accepted for bull train transport from Fort Pierre only after the barrels of fish and water were sealed so water wouldn't slosh out and spoil the other goods in the wagon. It was assumed that the water keeping the sluggish carp somewhat alive was refreshed at the various watering holes along the Fort Pierre to Deadwood Trail. Although they probably weren't on the freighter's bill of lading, the first false teeth were hauled into Rapid City by oxen in 1881. The story appeared

In the late 1870s, the newly established Homestake Mine in Lead City, near Deadwood, was in need of locomotive power to work the mines and extended property of the Homestake. Bull trains hauled this five-ton steam engine in wagon-sized pieces over 250 miles from the Northern Pacific Line in the Northern Dakota Territory to Lead. *Deadwood History, Inc.*

in Rapid City's *Black Hills Weekly Journal* on August 6, 1881: "There is in this office a set of artificial teeth found on the Fort Pierre Road some time ago. As we have at present no use for them, having recently filed up our old ones, the owner can have the masticators by calling for them." There is no later mention of someone stopping by the *Journal*'s office to claim what were then very expensive dentures.

Some bull train freighters chose not to sign contracts with large freighting companies. These freelancers would purchase supplies that they assumed they could sell in the mining camps and would freight them in themselves. One well-known shotgun freighter, as they were called, was the jovial "Phatty" Thompson, who freighted out of Cheyenne. In 1876, one of his loads was a passel of crated, road-weary house cats that he had purchased on the streets of Cheyenne for a quarter each. The cats sold well in Deadwood, the cheapest going for ten dollars, according to Brown and Willard's book

Black Hills Trails. It may have been some of Phatty's cats or their progeny that were enlisted in 1877 by the Northwestern Stage and Transport Company to patrol its Deadwood warehouse. In the January 30, 1878 issue of the *Black Hills Daily Times*, the editor described his visit to the company's depository: "We were shown this morning, as a result of their [cats'] labor, about one hundred mice, which they had slaughtered last night. The mice were piled in rows, waiting to be gathered up and taken for burial. The company estimated that the mice had been destroying from ten dollars to twenty dollars' worth of goods a day." On August 10, 1876, the *Yankton Press and Dakotian* claimed that the first Black Hills cat was "a genuine Thomas cat" that arrived in Crooks Town, near Deadwood, aboard a bull train from Fort Pierre. The month before, the newspaper reported that Joseph Pier of Yankton discovered a nest of mice in a bale of hides brought by the Yellowstone steamer down the Missouri from Fort Pierre. The hides had been delivered to Pierre from Deadwood by a bull train a few days earlier. Commenting on the arrival of Black Hills mice in Yankton, the editor commented sardonically, "The hills are in every way developing some new and valuable resources."

In 1880, staff members of the *Black Hills Daily Times* calculated the weight of everything—from mice, cats and fish to locomotives—that had been transported by hoof-power to Deadwood in the first nine months of that year. Only three of the six major freighters had exact figures, and the other three freighters offered estimates. The study found that 19,763,687 pounds had been carried in by freight, and that excludes the freight that had been carted in by independent freighters, which the editor estimated to be about 1 million additional pounds. As the population in the Black Hills grew to about 15 thousand, the freighting business also expanded. In November 1884, the *Pierre Signal* reported that seventeen bull teams loaded with 1 million pounds of Black Hills freight had departed from Fort Pierre. That cavalcade would have included about 350 oxen and about 50 wagons. In early 1886, the *Black Hills Daily Times* computed that the amount of freight hauled to Deadwood in 1885 was in excess of 25 million pounds. It was estimated that this amount was equivalent to what could be packed aboard 1,250 railroad freight boxcars.

It took strong, brave men and thousands of oxen, mules and horses powering hundreds of sturdy freight wagons to keep the remarkable and dependable hoof-powered supply train rolling into the Black Hills from 1874 to 1886. Men of vision stepped into the forefront during that era and led the dependable deliveries of all that was needed to smooth the rough edges of the Dakota Territory's western frontier.

4

THE FREIGHTERS

Favored with magnificent weather and consequent good roads, the several transportation companies are busily engaged leaning up the season's shipments with every probability of completing their contracts much earlier than usual or than was expected. On Sunday, November 9, according to the Pierre paper, seventeen bull trains started from Fort Pierre loaded with over 1,000,000 pounds of freight for the Black Hills, part of them for Fred Evans and part for the Northwestern Transportation Company.

—Black Hills Daily Times, *Deadwood, Dakota Territory, November 6, 1884*

From 1874 to 1886, hundreds of freighters using thousands of oxen and hundreds of heavy-duty, big-wheeled long-haul wagons accomplished what seemed to be the impossible task of transporting millions of tons of goods and supplies to the Black Hills. A handful of the most successful overland freighters climbed to the top of the heap and led in hauling what was needed for developing the Black Hills. The top freighting companies were the Fred Evans Transportation Company, the Minnesota-based Northwestern Express, the Stage and Freight Company and Downer T. Bramble's Merchant's line out of Yankton. Dozens of other freighters weren't far behind, including John Dougherty; Mike Dunn; Jewett and Dickenson; George Waldron; Fred, George, John and Louis LaPlant; Noah Newbanks; John and Joe Pattenberg; S.D. and V.P. Shoun; Louis, Israel and Joe Vollin; Mort and Oscar Sammis; and Ephriam, N.L. and Frank Witcher. The largest outfits used thousands of oxen, mules and horses to pull hundreds of wagons supported by warehouses, riverboats, loading docks and platoons of bullwhackers, muleskinners, talented carpenters, wainwrights, blacksmiths, harness makers, herdsmen and wheelwrights.

Hundreds of independent freighters were always standing close by with a freight wagon or two and enough oxen to power them westward, there to fill in when the big freighters were deluged with too much freight and too few of their own wagons and bulls to handle a job. During the busy months of the year, rather than have freight stack up in the Fort Pierre warehouses, the big outfits contracted with independent freighters to keep Black Hills customers happy. For a time, the freelance freighters went on strike for better pay per pound rates from the big operators, and they were moderately successful. The small outfits supplemented their freight business with government contract work delivering mail, supplying isolated military forts and bases and hauling food and other needs to Native American agencies.

As homesteading in the West and opportunities in the hills became more popular among adventurers and settlers, the tag-along pioneer families and others heading west sought the safety and guidance of the bull train freighters. On their journey west, pioneers would pay for a wagon slot in the bull trains' order of march. Freighters would also charge prospective gold-seekers and curious adventurers who opted to join the bull trains' trek to the hills instead of making the journey on their own across Oceti Sakowin (Sioux) country. With little in their pockets and heavy packs on their backs, pioneers would pay for a space on a wagon for their pack and for the right to walk along in the wagon's dusty wake.

By 1880, the best freighting outfit on the Fort Pierre to Deadwood Trail was Sioux City's dynamo Fred T. Evans. He was the first freighter to enter the Black Hills and was a pioneer on the Fort Pierre to Deadwood Trail, which eventually became the best route to the gold fields. Everyone in the territory knew, trusted and admired Fred Evans. Yankton merchant Downer T. Bramble started a freight line that ran as a close second to what Evans had put together. Unlike Evans's business, Bramble's Merchant's line waxed and waned, and in March 1883, he closed his Deadwood freight office and left to start a freighting business in the western Wyoming Territory and the Wood River area in the Idaho Territory. He later returned to the Dakota Territory for a time to try freighting on a route from Medora in what is today North Dakota.

The Northwestern Express, Stage and Freight Company started in Bismarck in the Northern Dakota Territory. After the arrival of the railroad at Pierre in 1880, it shifted its headquarters. The Northwestern's

Bull trains in the 1880s, which had up to ten yoke of plodding oxen, usually tied up traffic in Deadwood as they unloaded their cargo. *Lonis Wendt collection.*

affiliation with what became the Chicago North Western Railroad helped it eventually succeed in its quest for business. By 1883, its combined stage and freight business was the largest on the road, shuttling about three million pounds of goods to the west each month. Fred Evans, who avoided the stagecoach business, was managing a business that freighted about 1.5 million pounds per month, but he was doing it all on his own, without a close affiliation with a railroad.

Big Fred Evans's rise to the top of the Fort Pierre to Deadwood freighting hierarchy was predestined; he was a visionary and ahead of his time in nearly everything he undertook. He was endowed with restless energy and was as smart as a bullwhip; Evans knew the warp and weft of the freighting business. Evans stood at a muscular six foot four; he had a curly-haired black beard, his smile was his trademark and his handshake his bond. Evans could spew out the rough language of a bullwhacker with the best of the ragtag bunch, and the next day, could converse calmly in the mahogany-paneled boardrooms of business and industry. He was a public relations master before public relations was contrived. As his many businesses grew, his adventurous spirit took him far beyond the confines of freighting. After his death from Bright's disease in Hot Springs at the age of sixty-seven, the *Rapid City Journal* started the story of his demise this way:

> *"Fred Evans is dead."*
> *"What! Big Fred?"*
> *"Yes, great, big, large-hearted Fred Evans."*

This giant among men was born on November 11, 1835, in Parkman, Geauga County, Ohio, not far from Cleveland. He grew tired of school at nearby Hiram College and walked away at age eighteen, headed for the northern Wisconsin pineries, where he worked as a lumberjack at Big Bull Falls. Before his twenty-first birthday in 1856, Evans was on the road again. An article about him in the Sioux City Museum indicates that he left the lumber business and walked to Nebraska, halting at DeSoto in 1858. While he was there, he bought a few yokes of oxen and signed on to work with a bull train that was hauling supplies to the miners clamoring to Colorado and the gold fields around Pike's Peak. That experience taught Evans the "gees" and "haws" of the bull train business.

When they reached the Rocky Mountains, Evans and the other bullwhackers in the train found that they had been deceived—or humbugged in the vernacular of the day. The party held a council to debate their options:

Fred T. Evans, one of the most successful freighters in the 1880s and a successful businessman in other ventures, founded the town of Hot Springs in the southern Black Hills. *Chuck Cecil collection.*

they could either continue to California or set a course for Washington to the northwest. To decide which route to take, the young adventurers held a celebratory "decision party" of sorts atop Pike's Peak. Each man cut a pole, and in a fun-filled ceremony at fourteen thousand feet, the eight of them stood their poles on end. On a signal, the men released their poles, and the direction of a tumbling pole indicated its owner's next move. Evans's pole tipped toward Washington. According to an article in the Sioux City Museum, Evans left with five of his companions for the Walla Walla Valley, bidding farewell to the three bullwhackers whose poles dictated California. Evans took odd jobs at Walla Walla during his three-year stay. He chopped wood for a dollar per cord, worked on farms and ranches, and on occasion, broke broncs. He nursed his bruises and saved his money before eventually returning to Nebraska with a few fine horses that became the genesis of his successful ranching endeavors near Grand Island.

With his never-resting gumption and a gregarious personality, Evans's ranch prospered, and his cattle soon numbered more than one thousand. He was also successful in raising horses, sheep and hogs. The livestock business prompted him to enter into contracts to furnish meat and farm produce for the federal government and to the Union Pacific Railroad during the years of its expansion westward. Evans's captivating personality in the Grand Island area also earned him trust and notoriety. The Sioux City Museum's documents reveal that Evans was selected as Hall County's treasurer and was soon appointed to represent his county in the Nebraska Territorial legislature. Evans married Theresa M. Beal in 1863, and they had four children: Fred Jr., Frank, John and Ella. Today, the entire town of Grand Island, Nebraska stands on Evans's ranchland.

In 1868, Evans acquired a farm and timberland near the new town of Sloan, Iowa. He built the town's first hotel and became good friends with prominent Sloan businessman Ed Haakinson. The two soon became partners in a packing plant business in nearby Sioux City, according to the book *History of Sloan Township*. Evans also helped organize the Northwestern National Bank of Sioux City and served as its president.

He and his family moved from Sloan to Sioux City in 1871, when he was thirty-three years old. There, Evans bought another ranch and was a major stockholder in Sioux City's first horse-drawn street railroad. In 1883, with his freighting profits and income from his other investments, Evans bought out all of Sioux City's street railroad stock. Evans's oldest son, Fred Jr., managed that growing and successful business. Three years later, Evans organized a similar street railroad in Rapid City in the Dakota Territory. The cars for the Rapid City venture were apparently surplus from his Sioux City streetcar business. In July 1886, a *Chadron Journal* (Nebraska) reprint in the *Black Hills Daily Times* commented on the Rapid City–bound street cars. "Some articles, looking more like band boxes than anything else but labeled Rapid City Streetcar Company, passed through here the other day." The *Times* editor, who enjoyed taunting Rapid Citians and their growing community, added caustically, "Oh, Boom, of such infinitesimal claptraps does thy fame consist." Evans's Sloan, Iowa timberland furnished wood ties for the Illinois Central Railway that was laying rails from LeMars, Iowa, to Sioux City, a distance of about twenty-five miles. More of his timber became beams and boards for the construction of railroad depots and railroad bridges in that area, as described in the book *History of Woodbury and Plymouth Counties*. Evans also became friends and partnered with Frank Peavey in a Sioux City hardware and agricultural implement business. In 1884, Peavey moved to Minneapolis and became one of the nation's largest owners of grain elevators.

All was going well for Evans and his Sloan and Sioux City businesses, but his mind began to drift toward the freight business after reading about Custer's discovery of gold in the Black Hills in the *Sioux City Journal* in 1874. Rather than join in the fray as a gold-seeker, Evans had a better idea. Remembering his days as a Colorado bullwhacker, Evans envisioned golden opportunities transporting people, supplies and materials to the Black Hills in response to the rush that would surely happen. He figured he would mine

Fred Evans started his career as a businessman as the owner of the Sioux City, Iowa, horse-drawn street rail line. *Sioux City Historical Society.*

gold from the gold miners. Evans ignored the government's ban on entry to the hills and organized the Sioux City and Black Hills Transportation Company. The company dispatched its first wagon train from Sioux City in May 1875; the train was transporting about seventy prospective miners and their baggage to the Black Hills for fifteen cents per pound. Actually, the four wagons in the train hauled only the miners' guns, blankets, other supplies, and food—the passengers walked. "We started from Sioux City in the month of May, 1875," Evans later told a reporter from the *Black Hills Daily Times*. "We reached Running Water at a place called Garden City, where our wagons were burned by Major W.F. Walker, who claimed he acted under instructions from the government. This was in June, and the men went back to Sioux City, where the company was disbanded."

Later in 1875, Evans again tried to run the gauntlet to the hills, this time with a party from Dubuque, Iowa. However, the military also intercepted that effort near Custer on the southern edge of the Black Hills, and the caravan was escorted out of the hills. But Evans was determined. Although the Black Hills would not be legally opened to pioneers until after Custer's battle at Little Bighorn in June 1876, the tenacious Evans organized a third train, intent on making another foray to the hills in early 1876. Because he had already been arrested by the military the previous year and was known by them, Evans decided to place J.R. Gordon in charge of the mission. He instructed Gordon to proceed to Deadwood and return with the teams and wagons on the then little-known trail from Deadwood to Fort Pierre. Gordon was successful in gaining access to the hills and to Deadwood. According to a question and answer story published in the *Black Hills Daily Times* in February 1884, Evans stated that the party dug, cut and chopped its way through the forests to Deadwood and made the first road to nearby Lead City. The cargo was sold and the Gordon group headed east to Fort Pierre, where Gordon once again teamed up with Evans, just as Evans had ordered.

Gordon told Evans that the road from Fort Pierre to Deadwood was difficult to travel, and he was not impressed with it as a wagon road to the hills. But Evans elected to load up the just-returned wagons and the other wagons he had acquired and head down the road to Deadwood. With Evans in command, the caravan arrived safely in Deadwood, sold its load and returned to Fort Pierre to reload with the supplies that Evans had previously brought over on a steamboat from Sioux City. With those supplies, Evans and his group embarked on another profitable journey west. He and John Hornick, a friend of his in Sioux City at that time, organized the Evans and Hornick Freight line and commenced to do serious freighting business. In the fall of 1876, Hornick accepted the new company's task of checking out the freighting potential of the southern route from Sidney, Nebraska, to Deadwood. The trip did not go well. It took Hornick and his crew the entire winter, and on their return trip, a fierce blizzard slammed into the hills. The weather and periodic sorties from Indigenous tribal members on the return trip resulted in the loss of about one hundred oxen. By March 1877, Hornick halted his bull train in Crooks, a few miles from Deadwood, due to the attacks, loss of cattle and hardships caused by snow and cold.

That costly experience convinced Evans that their freight line should concentrate its efforts on the Fort Pierre to Deadwood Trail, but Hornick had become so discouraged with the freight business that he ended the partnership. At that time, the Evans line comprised just five freight wagons, but by September 6, 1876, the business had grown to ten wagons and one hundred oxen, according to the *Yankton Press and Dakotian*. By the spring of 1877, Evans had expanded his business and was expecting a shipment to Yankton of "two carloads of oxen...shipped from Texas" and "five or six [railcars] of oxen from St. Paul, Minnesota," the *Yankton Press and Dakotian* reported. In 1877, Evans intended to put at least one hundred teams on the road.

After those 1875 and 1876 experiences, which were trial runs for what Evans had envisioned, he became even more convinced of the many advantages of the Fort Pierre to Deadwood Trail. Evans acquired two steam-powered riverboats and commenced shipping freight up the Missouri River from Sioux City to Fort Pierre. He built warehouses on the west bank of the Missouri River, which included loading docks, derricks and all of the accoutrements that were needed for unloading river boats, storing supplies and loading goods onto waiting wagons. On April 23, 1880, Evans's transport system was tested when five riverboats that were loaded to the gunwales arrived at his docks. Within a week, those tons of supplies were on their way to the hills; it was an impressive accomplishment.

By late 1880, the Dakota Central Railroad of the Chicago and North Western Railroad finally arrived in Pierre, a tiny community just across the river from Fort Pierre and Evans's transportation facility. With this new, more efficient and less expensive supply delivery route, Evans purchased ferries to carry his freight from the railhead on the east side of the river to his loading docks on the west side. During the winter months, after the Missouri River had frozen over, the railroad freight assigned to the Black Hills was hauled in wagons over the thick ice. Interestingly, for these short hauls over river ice, the wagons Evans used could be overloaded compared to those that were sent for prairie travel. The *Black Hills Daily Times* once reported that one of Evans's short-haul wagons with a 9,900-pound load that was being drawn by "nine-yoke of oxen" (eighteen cattle) broke through the ice, but fast action rescued the cattle and the freight.

By the 1880s, Evans's business was growing exponentially. To handle the administrative end of his business and help increase his customer list in Deadwood, Evans purchased a building in Deadwood that he converted into a general merchandise store and office space. His store was called the Cole, Wolzmuth and Company Store. He hired William L. David as his company's agent to manage the Deadwood office, which Evans also used when he was in town during the summer months with his family. Evans was active in the Black Hills community and assisted other town leaders in organizing Lawrence County with Deadwood as the county seat. The *Black Hills Daily Times* reported that Evans was appointed as one of the new county's three commissioners by John L. Pennington, the governor of the Dakota Territory. Evans also built a two-story courthouse building in 1879

Until railroads erected bridges over the Missouri River in the early 1900s in what is known today as South Dakota, the only passages across the river were pontoon bridges in the warmer months and solid ice in the winter. This photograph shows a scene from Chamberlain in 1906. *South Dakota State Archives.*

and sold it to the county for $12,000. Evans had a good political sense about him; in June 1880, he was asked by a reporter from the *Signal* newspaper in Pierre whether he thought an eventual split of the Dakota Territory into two states was possible. Evans told the reporter that he was certain a split would eventually happen, and he correctly predicted that Pierre would become the capital of the southernmost state.

Aside from politics, Evans was also involved in the community's recreations. When roller skating became a popular pastime in Deadwood in 1885, Evans was a frequent participant at the town's rink. He also became a fan of the city's firefighting team that participated in tournaments throughout the upper Midwest. At the tournaments, the *Black Hills Daily Times* reported that teams of firemen would run races while pulling fire hose carts. As a generous and religious man who valued education, Evans contributed to many of the churches in the hills by hauling church bells at no charge. And in 1889, Evans established a $10,000 endowment at the Dakota Territorial Normal School, which is known today as Black Hills State University, in nearby Spearfish. The gift was equivalent to more than $250,000 in today's dollars. Evans was often featured in the *Black Hills Daily Times* newspaper in Deadwood, which praised him for his business acumen and community spirit. He was admired for his pleasant persona. In those days, newspaper editors recognized community leaders they admired by referring to them in military terms; in 1880, the editor of the *Times* began calling him Colonel

Evans in news stories. The following year, the editor must have become even more enamored, because he promoted him to General Evans. "He is a far-seeing man," wrote the editor on June 21, 1881. "And when a doubtful chestnut is in the fire, he prefers that some other paw than his shall pull it out, or at least try it, and if the thing is practicable, he will make a bold dash and appropriate the fruit."

The Evans line was hauling nearly five hundred tons of goods to the Black Hills annually by the 1880s. During that time, Evans trusted hundreds of men to deliver thousands of pounds of valuable merchandise, and he had lost only one load to theft. The *Black Hills Daily Times* reported that early in Evans's freighting career, two bullwhackers he had hired left for Deadwood with two wagons loaded with $1,400 worth of goods. The men never appeared in Deadwood but sought out a market of their own. Their teams, wagons and the freight they were hauling were never found. Evans enjoyed the trust that existed between his hundreds of employees and himself—he considered himself one of them. He started his career as a bullwhacker in Colorado, and the hundreds of bullwhackers that were a part of his freight line respected him for that. Evans's bullwhackers reciprocated his trust with hard work.

Soon, the Evans line had warehouses in every town in the hills, and Evans entered another phase of his many businesses. He signed contracts with the various gold mines in the hills that were in need of timber for mine tunnel support, smelter fires and rail ties for mine carts and wagons. In 1882, Evans paid for an advertisement in the *Black Hills Daily Times* looking for five hundred men to chop forty thousand cords of wood with a pay of $1.25 per cord (a cord is a stack of cut wood that is four feet high, four feet deep and eight feet long). At that time, Black Hills pine was free for the cutting.

Evans was especially interested in a new town that had sprung up out of the hay fields along what was called Rapid River. Rapid River was eventually renamed Rapid Creek and is where the town of Rapid City was soon challenging Deadwood as the center of Black Hills commerce. Evans envisioned that this change would happen and worked to introduce himself and his transportation line to the growing cadre of merchants setting up shop there. He soon became an active participant in the growth of Rapid City and was often mentioned in the *Black Hills Weekly Journal*, the city's fledgling newspaper. Evans gained a financial foothold in the new city by establishing a large general store with his brother-in-law. The Evans and Loveland Store was well stocked and had a price advantage since the merchandise for the store was delivered by Evans's bull trains. In 1880, Evans and other Rapid

A bull train pulling into Rapid City on the last leg of its two-hundred-mile journey from Fort Pierre. *South Dakota State Archives.*

Citians established a horse-drawn street railway company similar to Evans's enterprise in Sioux City that his son Fred Jr. managed. In 1889, Evans became a shareholder in the Sturgis, Deadwood and Bald Mountain Railroad.

At its peak, the Evans line owned more than 1,500 oxen, although, in her book about the Black Hills, Annie Tallent mentions that Evans owned 3,000 oxen. The Evans line also had a stable of 250 mules and dozens of horses. Those oxen, mules and horses hauled freight packed in the company's four hundred heavy-duty freight wagons. According to John McDermott's *Gold Rush: The Black Hills Story*, Evans employed about one thousand teamsters, bookkeepers, representatives and agents. The *Black Hills Daily Times* reported that Evans had expanded his company's reach so far that, at one point during his eleven-year freighting career, he was shipping freight to the Black Hills from Fort Pierre; Sydney, Nebraska; Cheyenne, Wyoming Territory; and briefly over the Chamberlain Trail to the hills, which he had personally laid out at the behest of the government in 1882.

That Chamberlain Trail was on a strip of land on the east side of the Missouri River that had been granted by the Sioux to the Chicago, Milwaukee and St. Paul Railroad at a cost of $22,000, according to H.B. Price, the commissioner of Indian Affairs acting on behalf of the Indian agent at Lower Brule in October 1881. The railroad was also granted permission to build six stage stations west of the Missouri on Sioux land. The Milwaukee line was also able operate a ferry from the east bank to the west bank of the Missouri River, which was owned by the Sioux. The Sioux dictated that the road could only be two hundred feet wide and if any cattle strayed beyond the road's boundaries, which were not well marked, they could impose fines on the transgressor.

The railroads knew of Evans's expertise in overland transportation, so they hired him to lay out the trail, erect crude bridges over small streams and smooth out gullies along the way. At one time, Evans was an enthusiastic promoter of the Chamberlain Trail, but his opinions evolved, and he soon abandoned it, putting his all of his efforts into his Fort Pierre–based business. When Evans was interviewed in 1883 by the *Black Hills Daily Times*, he was asked about the Chamberlain Trail, which he had mapped out.

> *Yes, it is the best road between the Missouri River and the hills, but when I put my trains on it last summer, the* [Lower Brule Sioux] *killed ten head of my stock because they got off the two-hundred-foot strip. This winter, I tried it again, and when the bulls got off the strip, they rounded them up and charged me one dollar a head for pasturage.*

Evans was always on the road, looking for business as far east as Chicago and New York. On those trips, he hitched rides on his bull trains and took stagecoaches to railheads for the longer journeys through "civilization." Evans was so familiar with the discomforts of stagecoach travel that, in 1884, he asked Deadwood's Mack the Saddler to fabricate a smaller leather horse collar that he could buckle around his neck on his stage travels. The *Black Hills Daily Times* reported that Evans used the collar to hold his head steady while trying to sleep on his journeys. On some stagecoach trips, when all of the coach's interior seats had already been sold, Evans would climb up on the coach's roof—called the hurricane deck—and hang on for dear life for hours of cold and often wet travel.

During the final years of his freight line, as the railroad approached the Black Hills from Nebraska, Evans moved most of his operations from Fort Pierre to Chadron. Among the bullwhackers he hired in the Chadron rail yard were several Native Americans. In May 1885, the *Black Hills Daily Times* of Deadwood commented on Evans's Native American drivers.

> *They were attired in anything but aboriginal regalia. One or two were wearing watches and chains, while the hips of an equal number were surmounted by a girdling belt well filled with cartridges. They handled their teams and freight as though familiar with the occupation, and immediately upon unloading, drew their pay and departed for the Gap. They were seven days on the road in and were accompanied by the ugliest bulldog ever seen in the gulch.*

By the late 1880s, Evans turned to the southern Black Hills town of Hot Springs, which he and three others established in 1881. Because of the natural hot springs there, Evans envisioned the development of a health spa resort with accompanying embellishments, including a lavish, three-story hotel named the Minnekahta. The hotel burned down in 1891, just as Evans was in the process of building a second hotel nearby, according to the State Historical Society. After the fire, Evans halted construction on that edifice and rebuilt his first hotel. This time, he made the hotel an elegant five stories high and named it the Evans Hotel. He also built what became the Evans Plunge, a covered, two-hundred-foot-by-seventy-foot swimming pool that is fed by the numerous natural hot water springs in the area. In those days, a swimming pool, especially a heated and covered pool, was rare. To this day, the Evans Plunge remains a popular attraction in Hot Springs.

Because Evans knew the owners of the Fremont, Elk Horn and Missouri Valley Railroad, he was able to convince them to add a line to his new town of Hot Springs. In the process, he also got a spur line to a nearby sandstone quarry he owned that provided building products for many of the buildings that are still standing in Hot Springs today. Evans generously donated land to every church in Hot Springs, he built the town's baseball park and grandstand and he personally paid the salaries of the players. For a time, he owned the town's newspaper, helped pay the costs of the town's fire department and funded Hot Springs's first brass band, according to an informative thesis on Evans written by Terri Hodorff. Evans was probably one of the most well-known and successful businessmen in the southern Dakota Territory. He could have had a successful political career, but he never pursued any office higher than the positions he had been appointed to in his younger years.

Another successful freighter and merchant in the Black Hills was Downer Bramble, who was born February 28, 1831, on a farm near Montpelier, Vermont. When he was seventeen, he went to Nashville, Tennessee, to work with his older brothers George and Gilman in the drugstore business. He later moved to Memphis with his brother Gilman and opened a branch store. According to Doane Robinson's book *History of South Dakota*, after two years in Memphis, Bramble headed west to Ponca, Nebraska, and opened a general store. He also married his first wife in Ponca, but she died six months later. In 1861, he married Martha Perry while visiting Connecticut, but she died sixteen months later. In 1866, Bramble married Virginia L. Vanderhule and they had two sons, Harry and Frank. Frank later cofounded and served as the board chairman of the Midland National

In June 1893, the arrival of this Fremont, Elkhorn and Missouri Valley Railroad passenger train to the southern Black Hills resort town of Hot Springs brought members of the National Association of Railway Surgeons. The Evans Hotel, built by successful bull train freighter Fred T. Evans, and his Minnekahta Block—a commercial building—are also shown. *South Dakota State Archives.*

Life Insurance Company in Watertown, South Dakota. In 1912, Frank was instrumental in the establishment of the Bramble Park Zoo in Watertown, which is still a town attraction.

Around 1856, Downer Bramble loaded a wagon with goods from his Ponca store that he thought might be suitable for trade with the Sioux and sent his ox team to Yankton in the Dakota Territory. By 1858, this trip proved to be a lucrative venture, and before long, Bramble had acquired enough funds to build a home in Yankton, which he also used as a general store. The house was located on First Street, between Douglas and Walnut Streets in modern-day Yankton. Bramble also built a warehouse in Yankton that became a shelter for the horses of Lieutenant Colonel George Custer's Seventh Cavalry command during their trek north to their new assignment at Fort Abraham Lincoln in the Northern Dakota Territory. In April 1873, while Custer's troops were traveling through Yankton, a fierce blizzard struck and halted the cavalry. Troopers were taken in by the townspeople once their horses were safe, as reported in Robert Karolevitz's *Yankton: A Pioneer Past.*

After the Black Hills were opened to miners and settlers in 1877, Bramble began freighting goods and supplies to the gold fields. He shipped his supplies upriver by steamboat to Fort Pierre, where bull trains carried the goods the remaining two hundred miles to Deadwood and elsewhere in the hills. Bramble also built a large warehouse and opened a small branch store in Fort Pierre. Later, Bramble pulled his freighting business out of Fort Pierre, and in March 1883, he started freighting in the Wood River area of the Idaho Territory. In 1884, he again became involved in freighting goods to the Black Hills, but this time, according to the *Black Hills Daily Times*, he picked Medora on the Northern Pacific Railroad as the jumping off point for his bull teams. That venture did not prove successful.

While doing all of this, Bramble also built the first steam-powered flour mill in Yankton. Julius S. Morton's *Illustrated History of Nebraska* also mentions Bramble's involvement in organizing the First National Bank in Yankton. Bramble was active in Democratic politics, and in 1884, while his application to become an Indian agent at Pine Ridge was pending, President Grover Cleveland appointed him receiver of the land office in Watertown, where he died of cancer three years later. After his death, Bramble was buried in Yankton.

The third of the big three overland freighters that responded in a big way to the needs of the Black Hills was the Northwestern Express, Stage and Freight Company that originally operated out of Bismarck in the Northern Dakota Territory. However, in 1880, when it became obvious that Fort Pierre and its sister city on the east side of the Missouri River would be served by the Dakota Central Railroad, an affiliate of the Northwestern Railroad, Northwestern's stage and freight line out of Bismarck packed up and moved its operations to Fort Pierre. The Northwestern Express, Stage and Freight Company was led by its president, Minnesotan and former riverboat captain Russell Blakely. The company he led was designed to secure a portion of the commerce that had been controlled by St. Louis and the steamboat lines for Chicago and the Chicago Northwestern Railroad Company.

Blakely was an innovator and made news with his major departure from traditional freighting. In June 1880, Deadwood newspapers wrote about a huge train of fifty lightweight, farm-type wagons that were loaded with supplies at Fort Pierre. Each wagon carried more than two tons of freight and was drawn by a single span of mules. One muleskinner managed both the teams and wagons with a trailing span of mules tied to the lead wagon. The system was called "jerk necking," which had the advantage of saving in muleskinner wages. The farm-type wagons were even sold to area farmers and ranchers near Deadwood at a price above the wagon's original cost.

After the original wagons were sold, new wagons would be ordered and delivered by train to Fort Pierre for more "jerk neck" deliveries to the hills. The *Black Hills Daily Times* in Deadwood predicted that the new system would "revolutionize" the business—it didn't.

Another unique freighting method was described in a story that was released by the *Black Hills Daily Times* on September 25, 1880. The story told of a train of wagons that arrived in Deadwood with two mules hitched to each of three wagons, which were all driven by one man. The Northwestern Company tried a similar tandem arrangement using oxen, with two yokes of cattle pulling a farm-type wagon and a second team of oxen pulling a wagon behind them. Both teams of oxen were managed by one bullwhacker. It was all the Northwestern freight line and Bramble's Merchant's line could do to keep up with the personable Fred Evans and his successful freight line. Luckily for the Northwestern, it had the advantage of also operating a stage line from Fort Pierre to Deadwood, and often, it could transport light freight on those stages.

Competing for freight business with Evans was difficult. In February 1884, Fred Evans was asked by a *Black Hills Daily Times* reporter about what he intended to do about the news that the Northwestern Express, Stage

Freighters unload in Sturgis. *South Dakota State Archives.*

and Freight Company planned to lower its freighting price to $3.00 per one hundred pounds from Fort Pierre to Deadwood. "Well," Evans replied, "as I have always been the cheap rate man on freight, I will have to maintain my reputation by making the rates $2.95 per hundred pounds." Evans always competed for business, and he was usually the winner in the contest. He knew the freighting business, and he knew about oxen, the mainstay of his freight business. He was also well known and loved in the hearts and minds of the people of the Black Hills.

5

THE OXEN

Yesterday was the worst day for bull trains we have had all season. They were thicker than democrats around a whiskey tree. If it continues like this many more days, there will not be a dollar left in town—[it will all be] *going to pay freight bills.*

—Black Hills Daily Times, *Deadwood, Dakota Territory, October 24, 1880*

The sloe-eyed ox doesn't dance like a high-spirited horse at the starting line, but the ox was the most dependable, most sure-footed and least expensive animal to buy and keep, and they were the best long-haul, day-in-day-out power source available in the late 1880s. From 1874 to 1886, oxen excelled in transporting the lion's share of the goods and supplies to the gold-seekers and others in the isolated Black Hills who were in need of supplies. The ox—or bull, as bullwhackers, freighters and others referred to steer—were saved from slaughter and allowed to grow bigger and stronger than other cattle. They may have lacked the sleek and muscled physique of horses and mules, but they had the temperament, stamina and staying power needed to keep the freight wagons rattling constantly across the prairie to the otherwise isolated Black Hills in the Southwestern Dakota Territory. Those plodding, cud-chewing beasts of burden were ubiquitous on the Fort Pierre to Deadwood Trail that became the most popular of the many rutted paths meandering into the Black Hills. Mules and horses also had a part in the early-day delivery to the hills, but ox power was dominant in frontier freighting.

Oxen cost about half what a good horse or mule would bring in those days, around $200. In 1876, the *Yankton Press and Dakotaian* reported that auctioneer Kee in Yankton sold a yoke of oxen and a wagon that had made the long trip to the Black Hills and back for $100. In the July 15, 1882 edition of the *Black Hills Daily Times*, two oxen weighing 3,400 pounds and a wagon were advertised for $200. In May 1883, the *Times* reported that the Fred Evans Transportation Company bought six hundred steers for $22,400; the company said the largest steers would be used for freighting and the others would be put to pasture. Oxen also didn't need to be strapped up with bridles and leather harnesses; a few dollars for a wooden yoke that never wore out was a worthwhile investment. In addition, when an ox's working days were over, it would lounge in lush pastures to gain weight before being sold to a meat buyer.

The cloven hooves of oxen were not shod to traverse the relatively soft prairie ground. According to a 1968 *Rapid City Daily Journal* article, it is thought that oxen on the shorter, lighter hauls on the rocky roads within the hills were sometimes shod with what were called ox cues, half-moon irons that were applied two to a hoof. It would have been a major effort to re-shoe an ox out on the prairie trail. Unlike horses, cattle have difficulty standing on three legs while blacksmiths nail new shoes into place. If an ox had to be shod for any reason, it had to be pulled to the ground and securely tied before the smithy could go to work.

On the road, individual teams of oxen did not follow other ox teams in-line because oxen have the ability to eat while walking. Spreading the line of teams and wagons laterally ensured that there would be fresh grass for every team. However, during times of drought, oxen may have suffered or

In this photograph, which was probably taken at Fort Pierre, a bullwhacker poses with his yoked team as they set out for the distant Black Hills. *South Dakota State Archives.*

The two "cues" of an ox shoe. While some oxen on the Fort Pierre to Deadwood Trail may have worn cues, the vast majority of the thousands of oxen on the trail were not shod. *Photograph by Chuck Cecil.*

even died from starvation on the prairie. In the summer of 1880, a drought stunted the grasses on the Fort Pierre to Deadwood Trail; freighters said the land was "so dry that it burned." The *Black Hills Weekly Journal* in Rapid City noted that the many freight routes in and out of the hills were "known by the carcasses of many a hardworking ox and horse." Leaving carcasses on the road where the animals fell did not sit well with the public when the animal's death occurred in a populated area. In the early fall of 1879, the *Black Hills Daily Times* reported on such an incident that took place in Elizabethtown, a small neighborhood on the outskirts of Deadwood.

> *An ox fell dead while passing through town in one of the freight teams, and to get rid of him in the easiest way, they unyoked him, rolled him to the wayside, and he remains there yet. The warm weather has had an effect upon the corpse, and it is becoming lively, and the citizens of that burg would like to know why things are thusly.*

Oxen, more than horses or mules, assisted with the settlement of the Dakota Territory's eastern farmland area on the Missouri River. Oxen brought the settlers and were used to break ground during the first few years of the development of the frontier. But as soon as pioneers could afford to, they bought horses. The Dakota Territorial Census of 1880, which was taken during the height of the Black Hills gold rush, recorded that there were 11,418 oxen in the territory. A similar census taken in 1885 listed that there were 35,991 oxen in use. Most of those oxen lived on farms and in communities on the east side of the Missouri River in the territory's more settled areas. Many of the bulls were at work delivering heavy loads of mining equipment, newspaper presses and all of the vital supplies for life over the famous Fort Pierre to Deadwood Wagon Trail.

Oxen can subsist on prairie grasses, so the cost of feed grain that is normally used to supplement the grasses was nonexistent. Horses and mules are not ruminants, so while they can survive on grass, when they are working hard, a daily ration of grain is necessary to provide them with the calories they need to pull heavy loads. Oxen could subsist especially well on the short, crinkly buffalo grass that hugs the ground on the prairie. In years with adequate rainfall, the oxen consumed even more grass than was necessary to pull their wagonloads, and they actually gained weight on their two hundred-mile prairie odyssey, arriving in Deadwood even more fit than they were when they left Fort Pierre. However, this was not always the case. In drought years, the average 1,500-pound ox completed its journey in pitiful condition; they would often arrive in Deadwood as skinny as a fence rail, tipping the scale at just one thousand pounds. After inspecting a team that arrived in Deadwood in November 1883, the editor of the *Black Hills Daily Times* lamented, "The cattle all looked as though it had been a long time since they had seen grass." The same editor commented on the condition of the cattle that pulled into town after their Fort Pierre to Deadwood journey in the summer of 1885. "This is the second trip this season from Pierre, and the cattle looked as though the roads were not all the way down hill and as dry as a bone."

Oxen are slow movers, but they are steady and can keep their seemingly nonchalant, swaying gait for hours on end. Horses and mules are not capable

A lengthy train of twenty-bull teams pulling two wagons each stretches into the distance on Rapid City's main street. *South Dakota State Archives.*

of the same. The U.S. Cavalry estimated the walking speed of its horses to be 3.0 miles per hour; mules walk at about 2.5 miles per hour. Meanwhile, oxen might reach 2.0 miles per hour on a good day, on a good road and pulling a light load. At 2.0 miles per hour, over good ground and without breakdowns, weather delays or any attacks from road agents or Native Americans, the trip from Fort Pierre to Deadwood would take ten to fifteen days. The journey from Deadwood and Rapid City back to Fort Pierre, which was usually done with empty wagons, was faster. On those return trips, some outfits would hitch six or more empty wagons to one another, load the yokes and chains of the other teams and herd the spare cattle back to Fort Pierre. This method freed up time for bullwhackers to hunt, relax and climb into a wagon and sleep on the return trip. The cattle on the Fort Pierre to Deadwood Trail were not the desired and valuable prizes sought by the night raiders and marauders; they were after the speedy horse. However, this did not mean that bull trains were immune to attacks.

The Sioux were always active on the trail, but their activity reached its peak in the 1870s; thus, circling the wagons became a necessity on the Fort Pierre to Deadwood trip. An account of the practice of circling was recollected by former night-herder and bullwhacker Charley Zabel, who was interviewed in 1932 for a story in *Outdoor Life* magazine.

> *At night, we camped at some good water hole or stream. The wagons were corralled in a circle, and the cattle driven out to graze. My job was to keep them from getting lost, or killed by wolves, or stampeding, and to watch things generally. I always had about two hundred oxen to watch all night.*

> *Just before dawn, I roused them so they would graze some before we started, as they worked better on a full stomach.*
>
> *Then, I rode into camp and would sing out, "Roll out, roll out, bulls in corral," which would bring the boys out of their blankets. The cattle were driven in then and yoked up, and the drivers cracked their long whips as we pulled out of the corral, one by one, forming a long line stretching across the prairie.*

As the threat of coming under attack lessoned in the 1880s, the practice of circling wagons ebbed. But if there were ever signs of road agents or Native Americans in the area, or if an approaching storm appeared foreboding, the freight wagons would be placed tongue to tailgate in the protective circle. This circle provided a secure enclosure for grazing oxen and prevented the separation of cattle during armed attacks or violent Dakota storms. On more peaceful trips, the outfits would sometimes form up close together in parallel groups, called wings.

Oxen are creatures of habit, comfortable in herds and perfectly content to be resigned in their place. They are, in their own way, intelligent and quick learners. The shouted "gees" (turn right) and "haws" (turn left) and the few other loud commands from their keepers, the bullwhackers, were their navigational aids. Freighting oxen reached their growing peak at age seven; until they were four years old, they weren't even considered oxen. However, from that graduation age to the end of their nearly twenty-year lifespan, oxen were invaluable assets to those who engaged in the cross-country frontier freighting business.

Since they were usually on the hot, dry prairie land west of the Missouri River, oxen teams walked from sunup to about 10:00 a.m., pulling their three-wagon trains. Each wagon in a train was packed with three to seven tons of goods. Oxen do not do well in hot weather, so around midmorning, trains would halt so the animals could rest. If a stream or a buffalo wallow of water was nearby, they were watered before they were turned out to graze until about 4:00 p.m., according to a story about the Fort Pierre to Deadwood Trail in the March 24, 1944 issue of the *Rapid City Journal* by Associated Press writer Alex Johnson. Once they were content and ready for more, the oxen, which were mostly lanky longhorns, were yoked in the late afternoon and urged on for another four or five hours until sundown. On the trail, the oxen were at work every day of the week on the nearly monthlong round between Fort Pierre and Deadwood, so walking in team became a comfortable habit for them.

A team's routine may change in wet weather or in the cold days of autumn. When deep snow covered the ground and the grass was buried, oxen were put out on winter pasture to fatten for the next work season. According to the *Black Hills Daily Times*, the busy freighters Louis, Israel and Joe Vollin once tried to stretch out the season for oxen and learned the hard way that the weather on the prairie can be unkind. The lure of money convinced them to accept a contract to haul flour and corn from Cheyenne to Deadwood in the early winter of 1879. Their train of dozens of wagons and 380 head of oxen got caught in a blizzard. Their journey was made even more difficult due to the poor conditions of the roads on that route. The sub-zero weather and blinding snowstorms on that trip resulted in the loss of 60 head of cattle.

Most of the thousands of oxen that plied the Fort Pierre to Deadwood Trail from 1874 to 1886 were Texas longhorns. According to William Hooker's *The Bullwhackers*, longhorns were known to be good workers in the yoke. Their legs are long and strong, as are their slim bodies; a fat longhorn ox on the Fort Pierre to Deadwood Trail was a rarity. Longhorns that joined teams were usually wild and skilled with their horns. One bullwhacker described longhorns as animals that were "wild as deer, and ugly." Ox teams on the Fort Pierre to Deadwood Trail could include twenty or more cattle, depending on what they were transporting. Teams of that size usually pulled three freight wagons in train, with the following swing and trail wagons equipped with shortened tongues. Wagons on the Fort Pierre to Deadwood Trail weighed slightly more than a ton when empty, according to the book *The Bullwhackers*. Wagons also had a cargo capacity of about three hundred cubic feet and could carry about three to seven tons of freight, but there is no consensus on freight wagon weight capacities.

William Borst, who was a bullwhacker on the Fort Pierre to Deadwood Trail as a young man, estimated in an interview in the *Pierre Capitol Journal* that an ox team's lead wagon would normally be loaded with about 8,500 pounds, the swing or center wagon with about 5,500 pounds and the trail wagon with 3,500 to 4,000 pounds. Borst said bullwhackers were paid around thirty to forty dollars per month, while night-herders earned around fifty dollars a month. Food on the trail, which consisted mostly of coffee, bacon and bread, was provided by the freight line. Game animals were a common sight on the trail and often provided crews with fresh meat. It was not unusual to see antelope and deer mingling with the herds of grazing and sleeping oxen in the late evenings or early mornings.

Guiding an ox team on the open prairie was one thing but controlling the cattle on the busy streets of Deadwood and Rapid City was another.

Navigating a twenty-bull team that was pulling three eighteen-foot-long wagons on a narrow city street was especially challenging. A ninety-degree turn on a busy, noisy street was a complicated pirouette for the bulls. The bullwhackers would call the square-cornered dance with raucous shouts and occasional ear-splitting snaps of their long, stinging bullwhips. Not all oxen that were comfortable on the prairie reacted well to sharp, concise city turns. An example of the problems of having several bull teams on the busy streets of Deadwood was mentioned in the September 3, 1879 issue of the *Black Hills Daily Times*. "A deadlock between bull trains, express wagons and other vehicles occurred on lower Main Street yesterday afternoon. They got so closely and tightly jammed in that it required a long time and a vast amount of foreign and domestic profanity to untangle them." In another instance from May 12, 1878, the newspaper reported, "Main Street was blocked from top of the hill to Chinatown yesterday afternoon with freight wagons. There was a deadlock at one time, and all was confusion and uproar, bulls were bellowing, mules kicking and bullwhackers swearing."

Contrary to what most assume, ox teams in yokes did not pull freight wagons by the wagon's tongue, which was also called the pole. To pull the wagon forward, a long, heavy chain would be attached to the wagon tongue near its pivot point; the chain would then be fastened to a large O-ring bolted to the bottom of each yoke. In emergencies, the chain would simply be wrapped around the center of the yoke. Because the oxen were connected to the wagon by a chain, bull teams could not move the wagons in reverse. Only the two "wheeler" oxen on the tongue were chained to the end of the tongue to allow them to turn the wagon. The two oxen at the other end of the team, called "leaders," were controlled by voice commands from the bullwhacker and initiated the sharp corner turns for the trailing oxen but not for the wagon. The two leaders began the turn with the oxen following somewhat sequentially in their tracks. As the wagon arrived at the intersection, the wheelers would then turn the wagon. The turn was made even more difficult for the bullwhackers by the two other wagons that trailed behind the lead wagon.

The oldest, most experienced oxen were called the nigh oxen and placed in the left bow of each yoke. Nigh oxen were picked as leaders because of their acuity, reliability and calm demeanor. They were usually calmer, larger, better behaved and able to respond more quickly to shouted commands. In the opposite side of the yoke from the bow nigh oxen were the off oxen, which were the less experienced animals, learning the ropes and routines from their travel partner. Usually, the paired oxen became psychologically as

The narrow streets of Deadwood in the 1880s were not designed for two-way bull train traffic. At least sixty cattle can be seen on this small stretch of the town's business block. *South Dakota State Archives.*

Bulls resting on Lead's Main Street after the uphill pull from nearby Deadwood. They are awaiting their turn as the two freight wagons ahead of them are unloaded. *South Dakota State Archives.*

well as physically close to one another, even during the grazing periods when the yoke that held them together was removed.

Cattle have good hearing, and the oxen on the Fort Pierre to Deadwood Trail learned to understand the meaning of their bullwhackers' raucous shouts. They were assigned creative names that they would be able to recognize quickly, because the bullwhackers' commands always began with the name of an ox. Some names were subtle obscenities, but more often, oxen were named after politicians, religious leaders or famous entertainers. Some oxen, as mentioned in the *Black Hills Daily Times*, bore such monikers as Beecher, after the religious leader and founder of the Temperance Society, Henry Ward Beecher; Susan B. Anthony; Mark Twain's gambling Buck Fanshaw and Tilden, which may have been after one of that era's Bourbon Democrats Samuel Tilden.

Often, turning the bull teams in the cities went awry. On August 23, 1879, the *Black Hills Daily Times* reported on a bull train that turned off Deadwood's Wall Street and onto Main Street. In doing so, the trail wagon carried away an awning and vegetable stand in front of the Washington Meat Market. In the fall of 1882, a bull train's trail wagon collided with a fire hydrant on Gold Street. The Black Hills town of Custer recognized the turning limitations of the ox teams. When the town was planned, its half-mile-long main street was made wide enough for the convenience of turning ox teams.

When climbing or descending gradually sloped hills that were considered by the bullwhacker and the wagon boss to be too steep, the lead, swing and trail wagons were unhooked and individually pulled up the slope or let down one at a time. If the hill was particularly steep and the load was heavy, two teams consisting of twenty-yokes and forty oxen would be hitched together for the hard upward pull. If a team became mired in mud, the same procedure was followed. In extreme conditions, when the oxen were unable to free the wagons, teamsters had to wade in and partially unload the barrels, crates and bundles and carry them to dry ground before letting the oxen resume trying to pull the wagon free. Often, in particularly wet places, the unloading and reloading was a daily occurrence, and the progress for the day was measured in feet instead of miles.

A general rule to follow when driving oxen is to use the same yoke on the same two partners and to place those same two oxen in the same location on the team's pulling chain. The procedure of lining up the oxen was related to their acceptance of habits and preference for sameness. For example, modern-day dairy cows, at milking time, invariably line up in the same order to await entry into the milking parlor. According to Rolland Johnson of Larkspur, Colorado, who raises and trains oxen, it would have been typical out on the prairie road to always have the same two oxen yoked together so they could develop a strong bond with one another.

The bull team's hierarchy, from the wheelers at the tongue to the leaders at the far end of the chain, started with the cattle that were yoked and hitched to the wagon first each morning. The progressively lighter cattle that worked ahead of the wheelers, called pointers and swingers, were added to the chain as they were yoked. The team's younger, less experienced pointer and swinger oxen at the center of the line were enrolled in something akin to an apprenticeship. If they impressed the bullwhacker with their intelligence and obedience, they may have slowly worked themselves up to become a wheeler or leader. Sometimes, however, they forever remained where they were in the team's pecking order. Worse, if they exhibited little promise as workers, they ran the risk of being sold for hotel hash. After weeks on the trail, the oxen became comfortable and familiar with the morning and late afternoon routines of yoking and the unyoking in the midafternoon. Most oxen, but not all, quietly submitted to the process

The ubiquitous wooden yoke was a simple, inexpensive device that worked as a replacement for leather harnesses, which were more expensive and difficult to maintain. Yokes worked remarkably well with oxen and even allowed one ox in the yoke to lie down while the other stood. These ten-yoke teams on the streets in Sturgis were hitched to three wagons: the lead, the swing and the trail. *S.D. State Archives.*

without strong objection. Difficult oxen had to be snubbed to a wagon wheel while being yoked. Oxen that were very familiar with the men and the procedure actually stood in line awaiting their yoke.

Freighters, as all good businessmen, were always willing to experiment with ways to reduce costs. An example of this was reported in the September 27, 1881 issue of the *Black Hills Daily Times*: "There were several big trains in town from Fort Pierre, and in addition to these, there was a train of fourteen wagons from Bismarck, each wagon drawn by one yoke of cattle, each wagon carrying 2,500 pounds. One man drove three teams." Despite this experimentation, the tried-and-true teams of twenty cattle pulling a three-wagon train proved to be the most economical.

As the needs and demands for goods in the hills increased, freighters bought trained oxen from homesteaders who had used their teams to reach their new homes and start their farming businesses. However, arranging for individual sales from farm to farm was time consuming, so for the big freighters, cattle were purchased by the hundreds, mostly from Texas ranchers. Rather than make up teams of only new oxen, the newcomers were placed in existing bull teams. These new arrivals were poorly trained, if they were trained at all, but with the exception of a few with bad attitudes, most caught on quickly. New oxen were usually broken in to the yoke by becoming a part of a team that was making a short haul from the Fort Pierre steamship docks to nearby warehouses, and beginning in 1880, the short hauls began at the rail yards at Fort Pierre on the east side of the Missouri River. These short hauls required the new oxen to carry the new supplies for a few miles to the Missouri River ferries for the trip to the warehouses on the west bank. If time permitted, new oxen would be yoked and placed in the middle of a team, where they learned quickly to accept the yoke and their place in the line. Eventually, the best of the younger, short-hauling oxen would graduate and be placed in a cross-country oxen brigade. The new oxen were always placed in the center of the bull train lineup so they could become familiar with the routine. Rolland Johnson said he often placed new cattle in with veteran oxen to teach by example. Johnson believes that the new additions would "definitely" be able to understand the bullwhackers' commands by the end of the two-hundred-mile trip from Fort Pierre to Deadwood.

As oxen grew too old to pull or became lame or sick on the trail, they were replaced by oxen from what was called the calf yard. Calf yard oxen were the substitutes on the team. The replacement ox would be paired with a veteran ox that either already occupied or was promoted to the more prestigious nigh oxbow. Older oxen that were too impaired to continue the hard work of pulling were usually put out to pasture to become fat before they were sold for slaughter. On May 6, 1881, the *Black Hills Daily Times* described the process more poetically: "Unhappy ox. What a wretched fate. Cursed and beaten by cruel men, you at last find your way into beef at the butcher shop." In October 1884, the Fred Evans Transportation Company, sensing the arrival of a rail line in the Black Hills and the consequential demise of the bull teams, began moving its old bulls to Evans's farm in Iowa, where the *Black Hills Daily Times* reported, "They will make the old boys fat once more....When the beef is up in the spring, they will be ready for the market, and if the choice does not suit the owners, they will again come under the lash of the bullwhacker and once more tote freight to feed Black Hillers."

It can be assumed that the ox yokes were numbered or otherwise marked so that, in the dim early morning light, bullwhackers, teamsters and other wagon train personnel could match the correct yoke to the correct oxen in just a few minutes. In his book about his days as a bullwhacker, author William Hooker mentions that, over time, oxen accepted the early-morning yoking procedure. "Seeing me coming out into the corral with my yoke or bow, they would come to me." As the morning yoking and evening unyoking took place, bullwhackers would be on the lookout for sores and injuries that may have developed due to the constant rubbing of the yokes

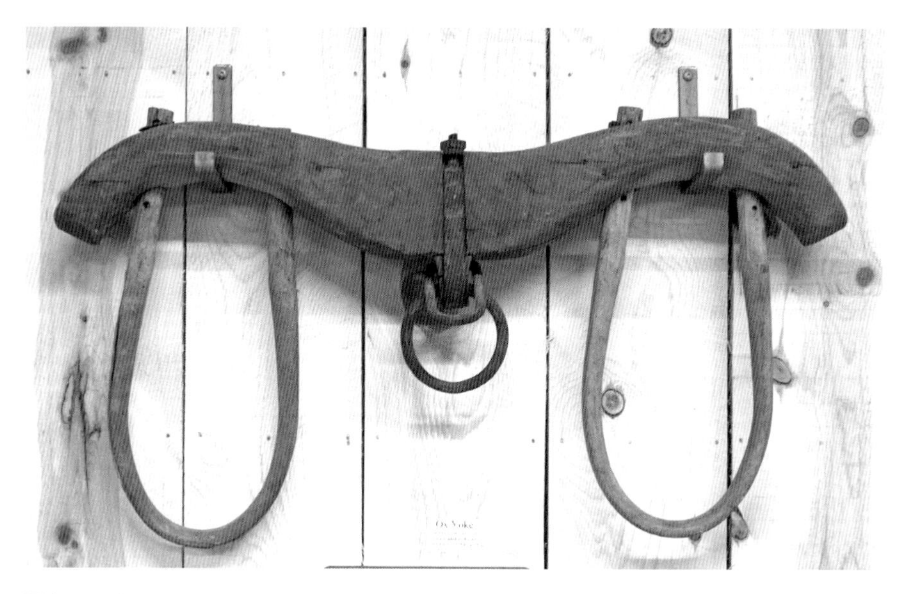

This ox yoke is on display at the Brookings County Museum in Volga, South Dakota. Note the large iron ring between the two ox bows; it was through this ring that the bull trains' long chain was threaded, leading back to a connection near the swivel point of the freight wagon tongue. This large yoke weighs about eighty pounds. *Brookings County Museum.*

and bows. It was to the advantage of the team owners to adjust the bow so that such injuries be avoided. The most common injury among oxen on the trail was lameness.

As industries and businesses developed in the hills, bull teams would return to "civilization" with wagons full of Black Hills lumber, buffalo hides, beaver pelts, flour and even gold-laden ore. On October 13, 1882, the *Black Hills Daily Times* reported, "A large ox train left for Pierre yesterday evening loaded with hides, pelts and furs of all kinds. Quite a number of wagons, we noticed, were filled with beaver skin." As the lumber industry in the hills grew, so did the loads of lumber that were sent east to Pierre. Bone pickers, including some peaceful Sioux families, made a living gathering buffalo bones in the Black Hills area for sale at railheads. In October 1886, the *Black Hills Daily Times* reported that Native Americans brought in 150 wagons loaded with buffalo bones. Each wagon was carrying around 2,500 pounds of bones that the gatherers sold for $12.50 per wagonload. The bones were freighted to railroads and shipped to St. Louis, Detroit and other manufacturing centers. The buffalo bones were crushed, and the powder was used in refining sugar and making glue. The bones also became buttons and knife handles and were used as additives in fertilizer and animal feed.

Writers in the West romanticized the life of cowboys and their horses, but the contributions of the lowly oxen in the settlement, growth and development of South Dakota has been mostly unknown. The late Doane Robinson, who was a longtime South Dakota state historian and author, was an abiding and admiring fan of the ox. He expressed his veneration for the animal in a 1922 address to the Minnehaha County Old Settlers Association.

> *For practically the first half of my life, the ox was a most important factor. The animal had patience and fortitude only exceeded by that of his master. The oxen transported the pioneer and his household goods into the wilderness, where he logged the land, broke the sod, planted the crops, then lugged it to market, and for the most part, made his living by the way, grazing the wild herbage between jobs.*

Robinson credited much of the success of early the Dakota Territory, and later, the South Dakota settlements to the ox. "Literally, the great human wave swept over the valley of the Missouri to the measured tread of the ox team."

6
THE BULLWHACKERS

What does a poor oxen get for his faithful and painful labor toting a heavy freight wagon over the plains and mountains? Does he get good oats and hay? No. He generally gets his hide cut open with a heavy bullwhip upon entering our streets by the smart alecks who want to show off.
—Black Hills Daily Times, *Deadwood, Dakota Territory, March 25, 1878*

Bull teams needed to be talked into starting, stopping and turning. Convincing a passel of oxen, often twenty or more to a team, to work in concert was the responsibility of the team's bullwhacker. Bullwhackers spent long days on the trail, striding in lockstep on the left side of their plodding charges, overseeing their every move and ensuring that each ox was doing its fair share of the work. While on the trail, bullwhackers quickly formed an opinion of each ox's personality and proclivities. The oxen, sometimes oblivious to what the bullwhacker was expecting of them, would be reminded verbally of who was in charge. The bullwhacker's booming, and often lewd, commands were shouted out and further emphasized with a hefty prod from the four-foot-long butt end of his bullwhip. If an offender was beyond the reach of the whip's sturdy and sweat-stained hickory handle, its frazzled leather end, which had a snapping range of about thirty feet, would be employed.

With practice, bullwhackers could make their whips crack like pistol shots. Many bullwhackers bragged that they could pick a fly off a bull's ear with the end of their whip. The intent wasn't to actually nip the malcontent but to get the oblivious ox's attention. There's a wagonload of disagreement on whether or not the bullwhackers would try to pierce the oxen's hides and draw blood, but odds are that in fits of rage, blood was indeed drawn. An article in the March 24, 1878 edition of the *Black Hills Daily Times* noted, "One ox in a team shows by the number of muddy whip marks upon his ribs, just as you can tell an anti-blue ribbon man by the color of his proboscis and the furrows of pain upon his whisky-pickled mug." It is possible, however, that the blood on the ox wasn't the result of the snapping bullwhip but rather the biting buffalo flies that often descended on teams with abandon and drove the cattle into frenzy. Only the oxen's tails could swat at the pesky flies, which are actually gnats that are about $1/8$ of an inch long. Once the flies found a team on the prairie, they abused it for miles. Great clouds of gnats particularly sought out the oxen's faces, especially around their moist noses and eyes, causing considerable physical and psychological suffering.

On the Fort Pierre to Deadwood Trail, the hardworking bullwhackers were each assigned to an ox team by the wagon master, or wagon boss, as they were also called. Wagon masters were the captains of the trundling, white-crowned schooners that slowly streamed across the Dakota Territory's sea of grass. Their word was law. Wagon bosses were paid well for their

This somewhat unusual eight-yoke bull team pauses on Main Street in Sturgis while transporting two wagonloads of hay for cavalry horses at nearby Fort Meade. *South Dakota State Archives.*

days on the trail, and with some experience, they could earn more than one hundred dollars per month, which was twice what the night-herders, bullwhackers and teamsters were able to earn. The wagon bosses would scout the conditions on the road ahead and spent their days riding up and down the long caravan of wagons, keeping an eye on their cadre of ten or twelve bullwhackers, the animals under the bullwhackers' control, the maintenance of the wagons (hubs had to be greased every forty or fifty miles) and the valuable cargoes being lugged along on the arduous journey.

Once their teams reached Deadwood, wagon bosses would supervise the unloading. Working with the freighter's local agent, they would help collect freight charges from the merchants before convincing the usually thirsty, cranky and road-weary bullwhackers to get their ox teams out of town and on the way back to Fort Pierre for another load. There wasn't enough space in Deadwood for a long train of twenty oxen and their three freight wagons to park overnight, so the trains reversed course and slogged back down toward the prairie. They would normally travel for six miles to Crook City, where camping and grazing land was plentiful. Many teamsters inevitably found their way back to Deadwood for a festive night on the town even though Crook City was also replete with saloons lining its muddy street.

Deadwood had its diversions and distractions for wagon bosses, night-herders, teamsters and bullwhackers. In May 1881, the *Black Hills Daily Times* indicated just how welcoming Deadwood businesses could be when bull teams lumbered into town.

> *Train's coming—the wagon boss with jingling spurs, broad sombrero and buckskin leggings is coming to town, which argues that the train drawn by meek-eyed oxen and the patient mule is somewhere in the foothills. When the ox persuader arrives in person, then will the dance house howl, the brimming fluid flow, the festive dance be red hot and joy be unconfined. Then will the "wooly horse who is hard to curry" amble about the ballroom floor, then will the "bull in the woods" bellow and the "wolf whose night it is to howl" set up his piercing cry, then will times be good and everything lovely "till the cash is gone."*

Sometimes, the responsibilities of the wagon masters got the best of them. Veteran wagon boss Frank McCarthy finally succumbed to his miseries near the Cheyenne River crossing on a hot and dusty afternoon while nursing a stubborn ox train over the Deadwood road, 110 miles out from Fort Pierre.

Bull trains returning from the arduous two-hundred-mile journey from the Missouri River brought back timber, hides and other useful products. The lead, swing and trail wagons in this unit, however, appear to be empty. *South Dakota State Archives.*

His assistant and the other teamsters spotted him "throwing freight from his wagon upon the prairie and indulging in other crazy antics." His mental condition was such that he had to be tied down inside one of the wagons, which was turned around and sent back to Pierre. From there, McCarthy was transported to his home in Yankton "laboring under a violent fit of insanity," the *Yankton Press and Dakotian* reported on June 12, 1880.

Bullwhackers were important cogs in the complicated hoof-based conveyor belt from Fort Pierre to Deadwood. They were usually young upstarts who were just hoping to make some money. Many bullwhackers loved their jobs and had a deep affinity for the prairie land. For others, a job at Fort Pierre was their opportunity to travel for free to the gold fields and excitement that awaited them in the rough-and-tumble Black Hills. The bullwhackers had the most physically demanding tasks of all the teamsters. They were always on the lookout for their oxen's long horns that would swing, either accidentally or on purpose, in wide arcs when it was least expected. Bullwhackers' feet were constantly stomped, and their boots were defecated on. In every way, the bullwhackers' 1,200-pound charges kept them mindful of their presence. On the trail, a bullwhacker would walk up and down the line of oxen. For every mile their moseying charges walked, a bullwhacker might walk two miles, back and forth, to ensure that each animal was pitching in. The herders worked nights watching over the oxen while the bullwhacker slept on the ground or atop the softest freight he could find in his array of three wagons. During the day the night herder also slept—or tried to sleep—atop the freight in one of wagons.

Newspaper editors of the day delighted in presenting the bullwhackers as dullards, bibulous drunks and troublemakers; they were reputed to be

The wide street in this photograph of the well-known freighter Noah Newbanks suggests it was taken in Custer. The ten oxen and disheveled wagonloads indicate that Newbanks, who was from Pierre, may have been unloading his freight door to door in Custer. The town purposely built its main street wide enough for a twenty-yoke team to reverse course in one wide turn. *South Dakota State Archives.*

misanthropic drifters. While bullwhackers' behavior at the trail's end could, at times, be celebratory to the extreme, the stories about them were often hyperbolic. In its July 27, 1880 issue, the *Black Hills Daily Times* reported:

> *A bullwhacker sailing under the euphonious title of Bronco made it red hot for them at the dance house Sunday night with his gun. He flourished it around and told them how bad he was and that he had come all the way from Fort Pierre to show them what he could do. The first thing he knew, Bill Dunn and Jack Manning pounced on him, and they done it so quickly that he was in the middle of the street before he knew what kind of lightning hit him. He slept in the cooler and loaned Judge Clark eighteen dollars in the morning.*

On October 6, 1880, the *Pierre Signal* invented a new word (its meaning is unknown) when telling about bullwhacker Frank Fosgate, who was on a side trip in Huron in the Dakota Territory, east of Pierre. "He was trying to run the town when the deputy sheriff held him up and he was taken to Yankton to languish in duranceville."

Some bullwhackers couldn't wait until they reached the end of the line in either Fort Pierre or Deadwood to celebrate. A Deadwood liquor dealer once complained that a bullwhacker had been sampling his goods while out on the trail. Among his shipment was a liquor box marked "East India Bitters." After it was delivered to his Deadwood saloon, the saloonkeeper opened the box of bitters, expecting to find liquor, and instead found a half dozen bricks, reported the *Black Hills Weekly Journal* on July 3, 1880.

A humorous column about bullwhackers appeared in the November 1884 issue of the *American Sentry*, a New York publication. The satirical yarn was written by former Deadwood reporter Jimmy Martin, and in it, he claimed that a bullwhacker's morals were "never under control." He went on to say, "In fact, I have often doubted whether the tribe has any morals at all, for it is certain that on slight provocation, or no provocation, they will render the atmosphere surrounding them blue and sulfurous with objurgations and oaths selected and combined from all languages."

Bullwhackers often did appear to be a sorry lot. Where cowboys occupied a colorful, romantic niche in the history of the West, bullwhackers, while capable, trustworthy and knowledgeable managers of cattle, were best known for a repertoire of pungent obscenities and foul language that would make a preacher blush. On the lonely prairie trail, this use of the English language was harmless, but on the busy streets of Deadwood and Rapid City, the shouted vulgarities were found to be offensive. At the trail's end, many bullwhackers eagerly and rudely elbowed their way up to the bar to consume extravagantly, gamble carelessly and fight recklessly. But they were also kindly and good men with a strong allegiance to honesty; they meant no harm with their fleeting loss of common sense. On the trail, they worked hard for their pay and two dirty tin plates of bread, beans and bacon—then called sowbelly. Bullwhackers and night-herders were paid between forty and fifty dollars per month, but the food they were given on the prairie could, from time to time, be very good. Wild game was plentiful and provided wagon crews the excitement of hunting and deer or antelope steaks cooked over a campfire.

Bullwhackers could be hell-raisers, but their youthful bumptiousness abated as they gained experience and grew older. Many eventually settled down and worked on ranches in the rich cattle country surrounding the Black Hills. They often acquired ranches, which they managed successfully, and raised good and respectful families. As a young man, bullwhacker James Rabdan moved to the West from Malone, New York, to live in Pierre with his older brother, who was an army officer. In 1877, at age sixteen, Rabdan took up bullwhacking. A few years later, he got into the cattle business, rounding up and driving herds to Mexico. He and his wife, Kathryn, raised two daughters together. He died as a successful husband, father and rancher at his home in Blunt, east of Pierre, in 1937, according to the *Hughes County History*. Gideon Larive, born in Canada in 1856, worked as a bullwhacker on the Fort Pierre to Deadwood Trail from 1879 to 1883. He and his wife, Philimine Varie, settled in the St. Onge area of South Dakota to farm and ranch. Larive died at age ninety in Belle Fourche, according to a report from the *Rapid City Journal*. William H. Borst, born in 1859, moved with his parents to Fort Dakota—now Sioux Falls, South Dakota. During the 1880s, he became a bullwhacker on the Fort Pierre to Deadwood Trail. He later worked his way up to become a successful hardware businessman in Pierre and served as the mayor of the city. Borst, who was widely known in Masonic circles, died of a heart attack in Pierre at age eighty-three, according to a report from the *Rapid City Journal* in September 1942.

Many bullwhackers succeeded in other ways, including William Henry Jackson, who bullwhacked briefly in the hills before becoming a celebrated pioneer photographer for the railroads and the U.S. Geological Survey. He was the first to photograph Old Faithful in what became known as Yellowstone National Park. It may have been Jackson whom the editor of the *Black Hills Daily Times* commented on in the paper's July 22, 1881 edition. "Among the bullwhackers in the city this morning was one whose mind is freighted with the pictures of the rosy side of life. He talks almost exclusively of daybreak, scenes on the plains, wild flowers and sunsets."

Everyone knew the bullwhacker called Shorty, but his wagon boss, Frank Whitney, was probably the only one who knew his last name was Updegraff. Whitney's bull crews also had a particularly tall bullwhacker they called Long Shorty; when he was asked what his height was, Long Shorty would reply that he was only five feet, eighteen inches tall. However, short Shorty was known as the more gregarious of the two men, with his self-deprecating comments about his out-of-proportion bowed legs. Shorty's height was even mentioned in the August 1882 edition of the *Black Hills Daily Times*. "Shorty, the well-known bullwhacker with an extremely long body and the shortest possible legs, was in town yesterday, swinging his monstrously long whip." In her book *Old Deadwood Days*, Estelline Bennett wrote of a chance encounter she had with Shorty while she was walking with her father on a Deadwood street. "'Hello, little girl,' he said, patting me on the head. 'My legs are pretty short, ain't they?'" He told Bennett that he had "walked 'em off whackin' bulls between Fort Pierre and Deadwood." Shorty also told her about a time on the trail when he stopped his bulls to wait for another bull train that had lagged behind. He was standing in the middle of the trail when the bull train drew near; the approaching bullwhacker turned his bulls in an arc, circling around Shorty. When Shorty asked why he had done that, the bullwhacker said that when he saw Shorty in the middle of the road, his legs were so short that he assumed he was standing in a very deep mud hole and didn't want his wagons mired there.

Former night-herder and bullwhacker Charley Zabel was born in 1860 in Sheboygan, Wisconsin. At age seventeen, the lure of the West brought him by train to Yankton in the Dakota Territory. The Black Hills were his final destination, so he signed on with a bull train in Yankton and headed north, up the west side of the Missouri River, to Fort Pierre. There, a freighter named Felix LeBlanc hired Zabel as a night-herder on a bull train that was headed for the hills on the Fort Pierre to Deadwood Trail. Zabel liked the work and the trip across the prairie, and LeBlanc found him to be a good, trustworthy worker. Zabel, who was called Longhaired Charley because he let his hair grow to his shoulders, became a regular on the

Former Fort Pierre to Deadwood Trail night herder and bullwhacker Charley Zabel during his retirement years in his hometown of Sheboygan, Wisconsin, where he operated an equestrian riding school. *Chuck Cecil collection.*

LeBlanc line and had soon saved enough to buy his own bulls and freight wagons, according to a 1933 *Outdoor Life* story.

In the 1880s, as his business on the Fort Pierre to Deadwood Trail grew, Zabel soon had a fleet of eighteen freight wagons and several hundred oxen. When the railroad reached the Black Hills in 1884, he sold his freighting business, married and bought a ranch north of Rapid City. Charley and his wife, Lillian Madison Zabel, had four children, including Nellie, who was born in November 1892. In 1894, a reaction to measles resulted in Nellie's loss of hearing, which sent the Zabels' lives in interesting directions, including a return to the old Fort Pierre to Deadwood Trail in the 1920s.

Charley's wife died in 1900, and soon afterward, he decided to sell his ranch and return with his children to his hometown of Sheboygan so his children could get a good education. Nellie stayed behind in the Dakota Territory and became enrolled at the South Dakota School for the Deaf in Sioux Falls. While her father worked in the Sheboygan Post Office and operated his own horse-riding school, Nellie left Sioux Falls and grew up in Yankton. She was married briefly to Dr. Frank Wilhite. Later, Nellie took up flying in Sioux Falls, and in 1930, she earned her pilot's license, becoming the first licensed woman pilot in South Dakota and the first deaf pilot in the nation. Nellie quickly rose to national fame and had an illustrious career as a stunt pilot during aviation's barnstorming era. She flew an Alexander Eaglerock biplane that her father had bought for her, according to the September 25, 1924 edition of the *Sheboygan Press-Telegram* (Wisconsin). According to the September 1933 issue of *Outdoor Life*, in 1927, Nellie took her father, Longhaired Charley, for a flight over the Fort Pierre to Deadwood Trail, which he had traversed so many times as a young man. Just eight years after that memorable flight, Charley Zabel died on Christmas Eve in Sheboygan. At his request, the former Fort Pierre to Deadwood night-herder and bullwhacker was buried in Rapid City.

The historically famous South Dakotan Scotty Philips, who is credited with helping to save the buffalo and who the town of Philip is named after, was a bullwhacker on the Fort Pierre to Deadwood Trail for a time in 1881, according to a report in the South Dakota History Collection. Cross-eyed Jack McCall, who was hanged in Deadwood for the murder of Wild Bill Hickok, was also a bullwhacker. It is said that Wild Bill's friend, Calamity Jane, was also briefly a bullwhacker on the Fort Pierre to Deadwood Trail, but that is doubtful. One of the most famous bullwhackers on the frontier trail, however, was a woman. It wasn't Calamity Jane, but a native of Norway, who was known by many along the Fort Pierre to Deadwood Trail

Emma Knutson Buckingham, the only female "bullwhackeress" in the Black Hills, poses with her famous bull train in 1887. Her husband's hat can just be seen in front of the lead wagon to her left, and her young son from an earlier marriage, Charlie Knutson, is riding horseback to her left. *South Dakota State Archives.*

as Emma Canutson (the name was spelled "Knutson" in the *Black Hills Daily Times*). In a May 11, 1887 article, a reporter for the *Times* dubbed Emma a "bullwhackeress," and she became known as the only one in the entirety of the Dakota Territory. The *Times* opined: "The most industrious man in the Dakota Territory is a woman. She was in town yesterday with a string of critters as long as Main Street and as scraggy as Old Rip's Snyder, and yet, she engineered the outfit through the city with ability, unloaded with alacrity and retired with dexterity."

On November 11, 1887, the *Sturgis Record* reported:

> *In the operation of cutting an ox in two with a whip, this woman's name is Knudson or Canuteson. She is married, her husband driving a ten-yoke team of bulls, and they both have been on the road between Fort Pierre and the Black Hills for six or seven months. The couple drive their own teams, about fifteen yoke of cattle with five or six wagons, and are reputed to be worth some little money.*

Emma was born Ingeborg Botne in Vinge, Norway, in 1856. She came to America in 1873 and settled in Minnesota. Nine years later, she moved to the Black Hills as Emma Botne and married Emmond (Armond) Knutson, who was also a native of Norway. The pair parted ways in 1888. In 1889, the diminutive Emma married another bull train freighter named George

Left: A formal picture of the Dakota Territory's only bullwhackeress, Emma Knutson Buckingham. *Minnilusa Historical Association, Rapid City.*

Below: Emma Knutson Buckingham, in a white dress on the left side of the photograph, operated her "hoofed" freight on the Fort Pierre to Deadwood Trail and in the Black Hills during the 1880s and 1890s. She was well known for her expertise in handling cattle. Her wagons in this Rapid City street scene appear to be loaded with buffalo hides. Buckingham died in Rapid City in 1902 at the age of forty-six. *South Dakota State Archives.*

The grave site of bullwhackeress Emma Knutson Buckingham at Mountain View Cemetery in Rapid City. Her husband George and son, Charlie, are buried beside her. *Photo by Darsha Cecil.*

Buckingham. They eventually retired from the freight business and ranched near Tilford, just a few miles north of Rapid City. On September 4, 1902, the *Rapid City Journal* had a rare page-one obituary that told of her death from cancer at age forty-six.

> *Thus passes away one of the characteristic pioneers of the hills. In the days of freighting to the hills, she evinced her sturdy independence by driving her own outfit across the plains, and wherever she went, she won the respect of all who met her. It was she who safely landed the* Journal*'s cylinder press at its destination on Main Street in 1885. When the days of freighting ceased, she took up ranching, showing the same independence and good judgment she had previously shown. But withal, she was a womanly woman, and her pleasant word and cheery smile will be missed by her friends, of whom she had many, and her passing away will be deeply regretted.*

Emma Knutson Buckingham, her husband and her only child, Charlie, are buried in Rapid City's Mountain View Cemetery.

7

THE WAGONS

Fred T. Evans writes that he will be here next week to begin the freighting boom for 1880. He has added two more large trains of the latest improved freight wagons to his line.

—Black Hills Daily Times, *Deadwood, Dakota Territory, February 26, 1880*

A heavy-duty wagon was needed to endure the prairie punishments that were experienced on the Fort Pierre to Deadwood Trail in the late 1800s. Freight wagons that were designed for the Civil War were improved and made into sturdy, wooden-wheeled containers that were able to trundle over rough roads with heavy loads to the Black Hills gold fields. Before the Civil War, most wagons were hand-built by village blacksmiths and wheelwrights. To meet the war's demand, however, wagon factories were organized and soon introduced mass production to the industry, replacing the slow and meticulous handcrafting of wagons. After the war, even with thousands of surplus military wagons on the market, many of the wartime factories began to produce wagons that were needed for peaceful purposes. The national movement to the West also created a demand for heavy-duty wagons that would be able to carry homesteaders, pioneers and their belongings to new beginnings. These iconic covered wagons were just the prototypes for the even huskier freight wagons that were later designed to carry larger, heavier loads over two hundred miles of poor prairie roads.

Most of the Union army's supply wagons were around 3.5 feet wide, 2.0 feet deep and 10.0 feet long. When they were empty, the wagons weighed about 1,300 pounds, according to S.E. Whitman's book *The Troopers*. After the war, the lessons learned by manufacturers in wagon construction and heavy transport needs resulted in ingenious improvements. By the 1870s, freight wagons were well-engineered and ready for long, heavy hauls. The wagons themselves weighed slightly more than a ton, and their high-sided, steel-strapped wagon boxes had a capacity of about 180.0 cubic feet. The weight that could be loaded on bull train wagons on the Fort Pierre to Deadwood Trail is a debated subject. For example, the article "History of Rapid City" in the South Dakota State Historical Collection mentions that "a wagon ordinarily carried from six to eight tons." However, a different weight was mentioned in a *Black Hills Daily Times* article from February 1882. The article, a reprint from the *Pierre Signal*, told of a transfer of freight over the ice from the railhead on the eastern side of the Missouri River to the warehouses on the western bank. "Two wagons drawn by nine yokes of cattle crossed the river. The lead wagon weighed 9,900 pounds."

An article in the *Sioux City Journal* from May 1880 tells of a purchase of Schuttler wagons by the Fred Evans Transportation Company. The Schuttler wagons had a weight capacity of eighteen thousand pounds "over any road." A short time later, the *Black Hills Daily Times* wrote an article about Fred Evans's wagons bringing an "immense wheel" to the hills that weighed twenty-three thousand pounds. The article said the wheel was purchased for use in a mine and that its two halves were each loaded onto Evans's wagons. The Evans Transportation Company also had several custom-made wagons for extremely heavy loads. These Evans wagons, many of which were made by Schuttler, had smaller wheels and strong axles, reported the *Black Hills Daily Times* on June 29, 1883. "The stoutest wagon in the hills is standing in front of Evans's office. It is a log truck [with] low wheels and warranted to carry, over any kind of ground, 20,000 pounds." More than a century later, one of these wagons that was owned by the Homestake Gold mine was restored by the Hansen Wheel and Wagon Shop of Letcher, South Dakota.

The dimensions and capacities of the freight wagons varied greatly, but the standard size of a freight wagon was eighteen feet long by four and a half feet wide and deep. Experienced wagonmaker Douglas Hansen of the Hansen Wheel and Wagon Shop said the largest freight wagon he has seen had a box that was forty-four inches wide, five feet deep and eighteen feet long. The rear wheels on standard-sized wagons were about five feet in diameter, with iron tires that were three or four inches wide. The front wheels were slightly smaller for better turning. Freight wagons on the Fort Pierre to Deadwood Trail had wooden axles. A wagon with steel axles, if they became bent or broken, would present a difficult and expensive problem for the wagon masters on the trail. William Borst, a bullwhacker on the Fort Pierre to Deadwood Trail, estimated in a *Rapid City Journal* article that the lead wagon he supervised carried about 8,500 pounds, the swing or center wagon was loaded with about 5,500 pounds and the trail wagon was usually loaded with 3,500 to 4,000 pounds.

Four wagon manufacturers dominated the industry: the Murphy Wagon Company of St. Louis, Missouri; the Studebaker Brothers Manufacturing Company of South Bend, Indiana; the Schuttler Wagon Company of Chicago; and the Louis Espenscheid Company of St. Louis. Most of the wagons rumbling over the Fort Pierre to Deadwood Trail, and those transporting freight to the Black Hills from other shoving off places, were made by one of these four manufacturers. But there are indications that some of the wagons used to haul freight on the Fort Pierre to Deadwood Trail were standard farm wagons and a hodge-podge of other composites. Some rolled along on unusually large rear wheels that were probably cannibalized from what were known as Red River Valley two-wheel carts, a model that was popular in Dakota Territory's northern Red River Valley at the time. In June 1884, the *Black Hills Daily Times* said that the wagons arriving from Medora in the northern Dakota Territory were "curiosities, their hind wheels nearly six feet in diameter." Many independent freighters opted to use the lighter and more affordable farm wagons, but these conveyances couldn't withstand the tonnage or the amount of prairie travel punishment that the gigantic mass-produced freight wagons could.

In addition to freight wagon improvements, there was a need for more efficiency in the freighting industry. Intricate methods of packing the wagons for maximum efficiency were developed, as were more efficient ways to quickly load and unload wagons, including the use of derricks, ropes, pulleys and blocks and tackles. The loading docks and warehouses along the Missouri River at Fort Pierre carefully followed a number of creative, temporary storage procedures and inventory systems that kept the massive supply of goods moving quickly and in the correct sequence to the hills.

A freight wagon's cargo box was made of one-inch thick, straight-grained, yellow poplar sideboards with white oak cleats. All of the wood on the wagons was treated with linseed oil, according to wagon builder Douglas Hansen. Because wagons had the possibility of encountering bad weather and due to the difficulty of crossing rivers, especially the Cheyenne River west of Fort Pierre, they were made watertight. In case water did filter into the wagon box, items that moisture could destroy or damage,

This photograph shows a refurbished Studebaker freight wagon, which was used on the Fort Pierre to Deadwood Trail in the 1880s. This wagon was repaired by craftsmen at the Hansen Wheel and Wagon Shop near Letcher, South Dakota. Note the hand break lever on the left side of the wagon near the driver's seat, which indicates that this wagon would have been pulled by horses. There were no seats on wagons that were pulled by oxen or by teams of more than six mules. Hanging from the wagon's rear is a chalk block, and on the right, a drag shoe, which were both used as secondary braking systems. *Photo courtesy of Hansen Wheel and Wagon, Letcher, South Dakota.*

including flour, sugar, blankets and pieces clothing, were packed in the upper layers of the wagon box, atop the barrels and boxes of supplies ordered by Black Hills customers. To cover and protect the cargo from the elements, a double layer of white Osnaburg sheets, originally made from strong, plain-woven cotton in Osnaburg, Germany, was used for the wagon's roof. The sheets were supported by six hickory bows to create an arch over the wagon that sloughed off snow and rain and provided shade from the hot Dakota sun. For added protection from the weather, the front and rear bows—or bonnets—were cantilevered out from the front and rear of the wagon.

Buckets of grease were packed in each wagon to make sure their wheels kept turning efficiently. A big dab of grease from the bucket would be applied to the wheel hubs every forty miles. When the wagons were empty, better wheel greasing could be accomplished. In 1932, former night-herder and bullwhacker Charley Zabel told *Outdoor Life* magazine, "When wheels were greased, four men took one wheel—two on each side—and lifted it while another blocked it up." Shovels for mud, gumbo and snow removal, along with spare chains, strong ropes and blocks and tackles, were also packed in the wagons. The gunnysacks that hung from the wagons' sides may have been used to hold dried buffalo and oxen dung that was picked up along the trail. The dung was used to build fires if no wood could be found at the evening campsites. With the constant use of the road by literally thousands of oxen, dried fuel of this type was never hard to find.

According to a report from the *Black Hills Daily Times* on June 24, 1880, some freighters adopted a new system for renewing their fleet of wagons; they began selling their old wagons in the Black Hills once they were unloaded. After the old wagons were sold, freighters would purchase new wagons at Fort Pierre and repeat the ship and sale plan in Deadwood. This unusual wagon marketing plan proved to be more profitable, because rather than take all of the bulls and wagons back to Fort Pierre for another load, they could simply sell their oldest wagons, or those that were most in need of repair, and their older, weaker bulls in Deadwood or Rapid City. The older wagons and bulls could still be of some use for the short hauls to the isolated Black Hills mining camps and small communities, but they were no longer useful on the long Fort Pierre to Deadwood Trail. In some cases, bulls were sold to slaughter for their hides and meat, according to a report in the *Black Hills Daily Times*.

It made perfect sense for bull teams on the Fort Pierre to Deadwood Trail to pull two or three wagons in a train rather than pack immense amounts of heavy cargo into one very large wagon. If a bull team became challenged by a steep hill, a mud hole, a stretch of gumbo or a river crossing, the wagons could be disconnected and pulled one at a time. There were cases in which stranded wagons would either be fully or partially unloaded by hand until they were light enough for the cattle to free them from the impasse.

In a two- or three-wagon train, the second and third wagons were equipped with shorter tongues that were hitched to the wagon ahead of it with what was called a "horn and bumper" coupling. The hitch was an ingenious device that slightly delayed the start of the bull team's pull, starting with the lead wagon, then the swing wagon, and finally, the trail wagon. This relieved the ox team from overcoming the inertia of all three standing wagons at the same time. The system was similar to that used on railroad car couplings, which allowed a line of cars to start moving in sequence rather than simultaneously.

The unique "horn and bumper" mechanism on the Fort Pierre to Deadwood freight wagons can be seen between the wheel spokes. *Hansen Wheel and Wagon Shop Photo, Letcher, South Dakota.*

Yoked oxen could pull wagons, but they could not back them up, which meant they could not scramble out of the way if gravity took over on the downward-sloping side of an incline. To prevent wagons from accidentally overtaking an ox team while going downhill, Studebaker and most other freight wagon companies included four brakes that could be used to help maintain speed on gradual or steep grades. First, there was the wagons' regular braking system, which was a padded block that pressed against the wheel. On slightly steeper hills, wagons could use a second brake called a drag shoe. Drag shoes were eighteen-inch-long, iron, ski-like devices that could be chained under a wagon's rear wheel. The drag shoe would slide over the prairie grass, literally carrying the wagon's chained rear wheel. A third brake called a roughlock could be employed on more difficult inclines. A roughlock was engaged by wrapping a heavy chain once or twice around one of a wagon's rear wheels. The heavy chain would then be fastened to the wagon, locking the wheel in place. The chain links that were wrapped around the wheel not only prevented the wheel from turning but they also dug into the ground and provided additional stopping power. Interestingly, a

The various braking mechanisms and devices are displayed here by a refurbished 1880s Studebaker freight wagon's right rear wheel. A chalk block is at far left, in front of the wheel is the drag shoe that could be fitted on the wheel, around the wheel is the roughlock chain and on the front of the wheel is the brake pad operated by a brake lever on the front left side of the wagon. *Photograph taken by Chuck Cecil.*

beautiful waterfall in the Black Hills' Spearfish Canyon is named Roughlock Falls. The name most likely came about after early freighters joked that the cliff over which the water tumbled was in need of a roughlock.

If a downhill challenge was extremely steep and perilous, a fourth braking system was available. Ropes and pulleys would be strung out behind a wagon and attached to a solid object, like a stone outcropping or a tree. In this kind of extreme situation, only the two oxen on the tongue would remain hitched, helping to guide the wagon as it descended. The other oxen were unhitched and led down the precipice. In an interview from February 1884, veteran freighter Fred Evans mentioned this system being used during his first bull train trek to the hills in the spring of 1876. "The wagons had to be let down into Deadwood Gulch with ropes. They proceeded around Poorman's Gulch to Lead City, cutting the first wagon road to that place." Entrepreneurs in the Deadwood area soon blasted away at the prairie and cleared toll roads, avoiding these steep barriers and other impediments, so the time-consuming and perilous rope-and-pulley brake systems were no longer needed.

On uphill pulls, if it was necessary to briefly halt the climb, two braking systems were available to anchor the heavy wagons in place and prevent them, the oxen and their valuable cargo from drifting backward down the hill. For stops during uphill pulls, bullwhackers could just apply the regular padded shoe brakes that squeezed against the rear wheels, but the wagons also carried what were called a chalk blocks, which were hooked up before taking on hills. A chalk block would be fastened by a chain and lined up directly behind one of the wagon's rear wheels to be dragged along on the ground, just a few inches behind the wheel, as the climb began. If the wagon stopped on an uphill pull, its wheel would settle back against the block, holding the wagon in place.

Most freighters preferred their oxen to have horns, which particularly aided the wheeler oxen on the wagon tongue. Because the other oxen in the team were only connected to the wagon by a chain for forward pulling, they were helpless in slowing the wagon even on the slightest of inclines. The wheelers, however, could, to a slight degree, slow down the wagon on very slight slops, because their horns prevented their yoke bow from being pushed forward over their heads. But if a slope had even a slim chance of being more

Wagon roughlocks were used to lower wagons by rope into Whitewood Gulch in the Black Hills. *Lonis Wendt collection.*

As a precaution, bullwhackers who were climbing hills on the Fort Pierre to Deadwood Trail with their teams would attach a chalk block. The block would be dragged behind the wagon's rear wheel to prevent it from rolling back if the bulls were stopped to rest on the climb. *Chuck Cecil collection.*

than the wheelers and the wagon brakes could handle, one of the other four mechanical braking methods would be deployed. As oxen matured, a lump of flesh would naturally grow atop their withers, behind the yoke. This was somewhat helpful in keeping the yoke in the most desirable part of the ox's neck, where the oxbow would be kept up against the bull's chest and assured the safest and most efficient pulling power.

Joseph Murphy's wagons were considered by many freighters to be the best, according to Mark L. Gardner's *Wagons on the Santa Fe Trail*. The wagonmaker is often referred to as the Henry Ford of his time. Some of his wagons were capable of hauling around five thousand pounds of goods. Murphy wagons were often referred to as the standard for plains freighters, according to Gardner. Murphy was a native of Ireland; he apprenticed in the wagon shop of Daniel Caster in St. Louis from 1819 to 1825 and established his own business in 1826. Some of his wagons were referred to as "Sixty Hundred Wagons," because they were built to carry 6,000-pound loads, as revealed by the company's specifications. Murphy wagons were meticulously crafted. For example, Murphy did not allow his workers to use augers to bore holes; instead, the wainwrights and wheelwrights used red hot rods to burn through the wagon parts that were to be fastened together. This method helped keep the wood around the bolt holes from cracking or rotting. Before his death in 1885, Murphy's company assembled more than 200,000 wagons.

Indications are that the Fred Evans Transportation Company, the most dominant freight operation in the Black Hills, used Murphy wagons for much of its freighting. Evans told the *Daily Times* in March 1880 that he had added "about fifty new broad-gauge wagons to his line," which gave him the "largest and best freighting outfit in the West." Each wagon was disassembled into fourteen components for packing and shipping from St. Louis, up the Missouri River, to Fort Pierre.

The Studebaker Brothers Manufacturing Company of South Bend, Indiana, started building wagons in 1852. And according to the company's published history, they started with a total capital of just $15. Twenty years later, the company employed more than three hundred men who built nearly seven thousand wagons in total. John, Clem and Peter Studebaker, like Murphy, also insisted on high standards. To prevent shrinking, they aged their hardwoods for three to five years. Most of the Studebaker wagons sold for about $200.

Studebaker's vice president, John Studebaker, visited Deadwood in April 1877, and he traveled by stagecoach from Cheyenne, which was 250 miles away. According to the *Black Hills Daily Times*, the purpose of his trip was to "investigate the wants of [the people] in the line of mining and agricultural wagons, and to look at the mines." In the same issue of the *Times*, the Studebaker vice-president talked of his firm's tremendous growth. He told the *Daily Times* that, in its early days, the company produced just five wagons a week; in 1877, the company employed six hundred men and produced one wagon every ten minutes. The *Daily Times* concluded the article by saying, "The gentleman under notice is one of nature's noblemen—genial, kind and as full of energy as an egg is of meat."

Illinois wagon manufacturer Peter Schuttler produced more wagons for the western migration than nearly anyone else. He set up his shop, the

Chicago Wagon Manufactury, in 1843, according to the company's history. By 1880, the company was annually producing more than $400,000 worth of wagons that individually cost between $200 and $250. The company continued making wagons into the early 1900s. The *Black Hills Daily Times* commented on a Schuttler wagon that arrived in Deadwood on October 4, 1882. But the reporter was either confused, lacked wagon knowledge or was writing sarcastically. The *Times* reported:

> *An emigrant by the name of P. Shutler—at least that was the name he had on his wagon—came to town yesterday with a long, heavy-laden train and turned down Lee Street. At the intersection of Sherman Street, opposite the farm, the trains's whackers were so intently watching a Chinese laundry worker that the cattle swung short off to the larboard and collided with the Empire Saloon. A back-up, a reef in the poop-sail halyards, four cuss words, and the danger was averted.*

Interestingly, there are only a few examples of those old freight wagons still in existence today. The world-famous Hansen Wheel and Wagon Shop has in its inventory an original 1880s Studebaker freight wagon that Hansen and his craftsmen were able to restore to the exact specifications that were used on the Fort Pierre to Deadwood Trail. Another 1880s freight wagon restored by Hansen's Letcher shop is owned by Deadwood History, Inc. and displayed in Deadwood, South Dakota.

8

THE PERILS

Just as we got to the hills, we were attacked by forty to fifty Indians [at] *about 4 o'clock when we were camped. We took the wagons for breastworks and fought* [for] *nearly one hour. We had two men wounded, and whether we killed any or many Indians, I cannot say, but they retreated and did not attack us again. I had a good gun and used it for its full value. The wounded men are getting along very well.*
—"Letter home from Chris Thompson in Deadwood," reprinted in the Yankton Press and Dakotian, *Yankton, Dakota Territory, June 9, 1876*

On the Fort Pierre to Deadwood Trail, danger was always just around the corner or on the far side of the hill. The trail was full of surprises, both man- and nature-made. The danger could have been the weather or the flooding of the Cheyenne River, or it could have been a covey of marauding highwaymen or a roving band of young Sioux warriors out for plunder, excitement or revenge. The danger on the trail never diminished during the decades-long era of freighting in the Dakota Territory. The possibility of death or injury always remained with the teamsters and the homestead-bound pioneers on the westward trek over the famous frontier trail.

In 1876, an incident occurred at Dead Man's Creek on the western limit of today's Haakon County that remains unsolved to this day. There is evidence that road agents may have been involved in the murder of four men, but Indigenous people were ultimately blamed. Dead Man's Creek is about seventy-five miles west of Fort Pierre, and it was at that lonely place of flatness and wilting grass that four young bullwhackers were sent back along the trail from the wagon train. They had orders from their wagon boss to find and retrieve a lame horse that the boss had decided to leave behind the day before. Sadly, Edward Saddler, William Gardner, John Harrison and Billy St. Clair were later found on the banks of the creek, dead and scalped. Upon a further inspection of the creek bed, more than two hundred empty cartridges were found. Headboards made from wagon parts, on which the names of the deceased were carved, were placed on a mass grave near the crossing of what became Dead Man's Creek. The people who found the bodies assumed they had been victims of a Oceti Sakowin (Sioux) attack, but a few months after the incident, someone in Montana spotted four branded mules that had been used to draw the men's wagon to the creek. According to Virginia Driving Hawk Sneve's book *South Dakota Geographic Names*, this sighting convinced many Dakotans that the murderers at Dead Man's Creek were probably not Sioux.

In another incident, road agent Persimmons Bill, who was known to travel with Native American renegades, was involved in one of the most heinous attacks to occur in the Black Hills area, as described in the South Dakota Historical Collection. In early 1876, a teamster named Simpson was transporting successful baker and part-time gold miner Charles Metz; his wife, Rachel; and an African American cook from Custer back to their home in Laramie. The party stopped for lunch in Red Canyon, which was just a dozen miles south of Custer, when Native Americans, along with Persimmons Bill, attacked the party in what was described as a "bloody harvest." The teamster, the cook and the Metzes were all killed. The Metzes' wagon was ransacked; the cash and gold that Charles was carrying was missing, but the Sioux had no use for it, investigators surmised. It was assumed that they were after good horses, guns, food, supplies and other interesting and useful pieces of the white man's curiosities. Only Persimmons Bill and his fellow white ne'er-do-wells knew the value of the greenbacks and gold stashed in the Metzes' wagon.

On July 17, 1877, on the Bismarck Trail, which was near Bear Butte and Sturgis and a few miles north of the Fort Pierre to Deadwood Trail, two brothers and one of their wives, were returning to civilization after spending all of their money in a quest for gold. As they were leaving the hills and making good time on the prairie east of Bear Butte, they were ambushed and killed. The attackers scalped all three of the men and cut the throats of their oxen, the *Yankton Press and Dakotian* reported.

Local historians have placed protective pipes around an old grave marker that was placed at the site of the murder of four bullwhackers who were sent back along the Fort Pierre to Deadwood Trail to search for a lame horse they had left behind earlier. Native Americans were blamed for the men's demise, but later findings indicated that the men may have been killed by road agents disguised as Sioux warriors. The mass grave marker is just one of fifty-two that Roy and Edith Norman of Hayes made and placed along the Fort Pierre to Deadwood Trail. *Lonis Wendt collection.*

On a grassy hill near Rapid City, another violent event is marked for history. A simple monument honors the memory of a young and adventurous pioneer named William Coogan. He was headed for the gold fields just weeks before the Battle of Little Bighorn took place on what the Oceti Sakowin called the Greasy Grass. In April 1876, for the last leg of his long journey from his home in Watertown, Wisconsin, Coogan had the good luck to hitch a ride with a hills-bound bull team in Fort Pierre. It was common for gold-seekers who were walking to the hills to pay a dollar or two for the privilege of walking along in the bull train's dust. Coogan tossed his rucksack into one of the train's wagons and walked along with the bullwhacker. After the slow-moving train had forded the Cheyenne River and slogged out of the river's valley near the little town of Smithville—north of what is today the town of Wasta—Coogan could just make out, for the first time, the distant Black Hills shimmering on the horizon. He decided to leave the slow-moving bull team and walk the remaining thirty-five or forty miles alone. This turned out to be a fateful mistake. On May 4, 1876, a few miles east of Rapid City, close to what is today Interstate 90, Sioux warriors killed him.

The diary of John Brennan, one of the founders of Rapid City, was quoted by the Associated Press in a *Watertown Public Opinion* (South Dakota) article about Coogan from October 9, 1965. Brennan's diary, as noted by the article, said Coogan was killed with a tomahawk before being scalped and having his ears cut off. Brennan's diary also mentions that the bullwhackers from the wagon train he had left near the Cheyenne River found the body and reported its location to Rapid City authorities. Authorities went to the site, found the body and buried Coogan there. More than a century later, when Interstate Highway 90 was being constructed, the contractor was alerted to the grave site's location as his work approached the area. After some careful digging, the operator of a bulldozer found the grave, and Coogan's remains were moved to a new location not far from the highway's route. In 2017, the *Rapid City Journal* reported that a young man named Luke Eisenbraun researched the story and had a large boulder and sign placed at Coogan's prairie grave site for his Rapid City Eagle Scout project.

Coogan's killing appeared to be related to a May 2, 1876 "letter to the editor" that was sent to the *Yankton Press and Dakotian*. When Addison Brooks wrote to his mother in Yankton, he told her about his journey to the gold fields. "About a mile from this place [Rapid City], we saw a new-made grave. Upon the headboard was the inscription: 'William Cowan. Killed by Indians. Buried April 26, 1876.'" But Brooks was mistaken; he had confused Coogan's death with that of a man named Cowan. Around mid-August of the same year, months after Brooks's letter home in May, a man named William Cowan was indeed found dead near Deadwood, according to a report from the *Yankton Press and Dakotian*. An inquest was held regarding the death of Cowan, who was found to be a forty-year-old printer from St. Joseph, Missouri. It was ruled that the "deceased came to his death by the excessive use of intoxicating liquor and exposure."

Around two months after the destruction of the Seventh Cavalry at the Battle of Little Bighorn, pony express rider Charles "Red" Nolin was nearing the end of his ride along the eastern edge of the Black Hills. On the evening of August 19, 1879, the twenty-four-year-old bullwhacker turned express rider was killed by the Sioux in what is today Sturgis, South Dakota. He was part of a team of riders that carried mail from Fort Pierre to Deadwood over the same well-used wagon road that Coogan had been

Gold-seeker William Coogan hitched a ride with a bull train that was leaving Fort Pierre for the Black Hills in 1876. After the bull train crossed the Cheyenne River at Smithville, Coogan decided he could walk faster than the bulls and left the protection of the group. On May 4, 1876, Coogan was killed and scalped by Native Americans at this site near Rapid City, ending his dreams of striking it rich. *Photograph by Robert Cecil.*

on with his bull team escort. Earlier on that fateful day, Nolin and his lathered horse passed a group of bull team freighters along the banks of Alkali Creek. The freighters warned him that there were hostiles in the area and invited him to camp for the night with them. Nolin declined, saying he was eager to complete his mail run; he'd promised his mother he would return home once the work was done. His mutilated body was found the next morning on what is today Junction Avenue in Sturgis. On the day Nolin's body was found, Henry Weston Smith, known in Deadwood's lore as Preacher Smith, was killed south of Deadwood. Hostile warriors,

This monument was erected in Sturgis to honor the memory of Charles "Red" Nolin, a twenty-four-year-old bullwhacker turned pony mail carrier who was ambushed and killed in Sturgis in August 1876. *Photograph by Robert Cecil.*

perhaps the same warriors who killed Nolin, were blamed for the minister's demise, although this was never proven.

The events that brought Clark Pelton, also known as the Kid, to the forefront were never doubted by anyone. On May 19, 1879, the *Black Hills Daily Times* reported that Pelton and a man known as Laughing Sam were among a party that robbed Henry Homan's freight outfit as it was returning to Pierre from the Black Hills by way of the Elkhorn Valley in 1877. The Kid was wanted for robbing stagecoaches and freighters on the trail, but he was also later arrested and charged with the murder of Deputy Sheriff Kuony at Six Mile Ranch, just below Fort Laramie. Kuony was attempting to arrest the Kid and Laughing Sam for horse theft, but somehow, during the return trip to Laramie, the Kid grabbed Kuony's pistol and shot him.

In the June 22, 1876 issue of the *Yankton Press and Dakotian*, a letter to the editor from a Fort Pierre observer told of three natives who were killed a short distance from Fort Pierre by gold-seekers who were on their way to the hills. A few months later, the *Dakotian* also reported "a deserted ranch on the sand hill route contained this announcement written on the four of clubs that had been nailed to the ranch house door: 'Indians too thick. We can't stay.'"

Peno Springs was a delightful stopping place for the bull trains in the early days of freighting in the Black Hills. Near the springs, a freighter named Edmond (probably Armond) Knudson and his bull train were attacked on August 21, 1879, by what Knudson thought was a group of three Sioux Oceti Sakowin. When Knudson and his bull train arrived in Deadwood a week later, the bullet holes in his wagons and the damaged merchandise were evident. The *Black Hills Daily Times* said that a store display case ordered by N. Hattenbach "was struck twice and mashed into smithereens." Fortunately, Knudson was not injured.

Violence was prevalent on all of the routes leading into the Black Hills, especially the southern route from Sidney, Nebraska. The attacks seemed to be concentrated on the roads into the hills and out on the prairie foothills. Rather than being cornered in the canyons of Black Hills or penned up in unfamiliar hills territory, attackers picked the flatter, less timbered lands that offered a variety of hiding places and escape routes. But attacks could occur anywhere. In 1876, when a recently arrived miner named J.W. Owens was writing from Whitewood in the hills to his friends back home in Yankton, he advised, "Any parties coming to the hills want to get in a big crowd with plenty of guns and a few cannons and good sand [powder] to back it up." At that time, it was estimated that about six thousand miners were at work in the creeks around Deadwood and Whitewood. In an October 22, 1876 report in the *Yankton Press and Dakotian*, the community of Deadwood alone was reported to have a population around 3,900 people.

Deadwood area miners and others were particularly disturbed by a report in Deadwood newspapers in mid-February 1877 that recounted simultaneous attacks by Native Americans that led to "the feeling that the Indians [were] surrounding [the] vicinity." The story mentioned an attack on Pierre freighter Vollin's bull trains near Bear Butte, and it also reported, "Wigginton's herd of horses, which was near Crook City, all were captured, Wigginton wounded and his assistant killed. Considerable stock in the vicinity of Spearfish was also run off." On February 13, 1879, two bullwhackers were killed by the Sioux near what was called the Madden Ranch, a stage station west of the Cheyenne River, according to a report in the *Black Hills Weekly Journal*. The bullwhackers were having difficulty getting their wagonloads uphill and out of the river valley's west side; they were attacked as they were partially unloading one of the wagons to lighten it enough for a team to pull it up the incline. While they were working, they failed to see their opponents approaching. Bullwhacker James Brady was shot twice; the first bullet struck him below his shoulder blade. He managed to run for about thirty yards before a second shot struck him in the temple, killing him instantly. He was not scalped, but firewood was piled over his body, and he was partially cremated. His partner, Frank Hannon, was shot in the abdomen, and he managed to crawl to the Madden Ranch. Before his death, Hannon had requested that his body be returned to Dubuque, Iowa, where his family lived. Bullwhacker Charley Zabel and others found Brady's body, the partially burned wagons and their cargo of grain bags that were ripped open and strewn over the prairie. "They never had a chance," said Brady.

A week later, on February 22, 1879, near the trail's same Rapid City fork, two more bullwhackers, S.D. Reed and Joe Pitt, who were hauling goods bound for the Evans and Loveland General Store in Rapid City, were looking forward to reaching their destination early the next morning. Each man was in charge of a wagon and a trail wagon. In the early evening, they noticed a small band of Sioux following them. They stopped to consider what they should do, and they counted twelve Sioux that, at one time, came within one hundred yards of them. The Sioux were wearing new red shirts, indicating that they had very recently received annuity goods, probably from the Red Cloud Agency. Reed and Pitt concluded that the Native Americans would not bother them during the night but that they would probably make an attack at daybreak. They decided that they would wait until dark, when Reed would set out on foot for Rapid City to find help. After nightfall, Reed left Pitt and made it safely to Rapid City. Within an hour and a half, more than a dozen well-armed men galloped out of Rapid City and escorted the Evans Transportation wagons and the men into town. After Reed reported that the Native Americans were six miles away, the *Black Hills Weekly Journal* picked up what transpired.

> *"Fatty" Madden, who can "transfigrify" himself from a glib-tongued commercial traveler to a heavyweight fighting man whenever the emergency requires, accompanied by Chris Jensen, at once started off behind a fast team for Fort Meade; and by noon the next day, two companies of cavalry galloped into town under command of Captain French. The troops gave their horses about two hours rest, then started down the Pierre road but did not arrive at Washta Spring Ranch until nine o'clock the next morning. They had a supply train with them and a week's rations.*

The *Black Hills Weekly Journal* opined in its March 1, 1879 report of the incident, "Had the command arrived at the Washta Spring Ranch by four o'clock in the afternoon of the day they arrived here, they would have had the fun of an engagement for all that day until that hour the Indians were storming that point."

Related to this February 1879 account of freighters Reed and Pitt was an interesting story that appeared in the *Black Hills Weekly Journal*. It told of an escape from what was apparently the same band of warriors who were intending to attack the Reed and Pitt bull team wagons. Veteran Fort Pierre freighter M.V. Shoun, who was in Deadwood at the time, had bull trains en route to Fort Pierre from the Cheyenne River. He had heard about the trouble with the Sioux on the trail between the Cheyenne River and Rapid City and set out to catch up with his wagons and alert them of possible trouble ahead. The following account of that adventure appeared in the *Black Hills Weekly Journal* on March 1, 1879:

> *From Hugh Morrison, who owns the Washta Spring Ranch seventeen miles out from Rapid City on the Pierre Road, we get the full particulars of a desperate attack by nine Indians upon M.V. Shoun, the well-known freighter and his hair-breath escape.*
>
> *The attack was made on Saturday morning,* [February 22, 1879], *when Mr. Shoun, on foot, was on his way down to his team camped on the*

Cheyenne. He had come through from Crook City alone, having heard of the Indian troubles, to hurry his train on down to the Missouri River beyond the reach of danger.

About two and a half miles from Mr. Morrison's ranch, between the Main Rapid City Road and the Witcher cut-off about sunrise, Mr. Shoun discovered a party of Indians advancing upon him at a distance of about three-quarter of a mile, the discovery first being made by the reflection of the sun's rays from their gun barrels.

The Indians were between him and the ranch, making it impossible to retreat in that direction. So, he ran away in the direction of Rapid City Road, looking as he went for an advantage point to make a stand to fight or conceal himself in. He at last found a deep depression in the prairie with large boulders strewn around in profusion.

The bullets whistled by him in dangerous proximity as he threw himself into the natural defense. He had no rifle but was armed with two large-sized revolvers for which he had sixty-five cartridges. He at once opened fire on the Indians, checking their advance for a time, which time he improved in hastily, constructing from the surrounding boulders a bullet-proof wall around the hole.

Through the opening between the rocks, he could shoot, but the Indians continued to advance until they came near enough to throw stones within his little fortification.

Mr. Shoun could not take aim and thinks he did not kill any of the Indians, though he believes he wounded one of their horses. After continuing the attack for four hours, the Indians fired the prairie, which was heavily covered with dry grass, and he certainly would have been driven out by the advancing flames had he not had the courage and forethought to reach over the rim of the hole he was in and pull up all the big grass within reach; and then, when the fire came close enough, he beat it out with his overcoat, a shower of bullets being discharged at him each time he struck with the coat.

These tactics were continued until the prairie was burned bare all around him, and he was out of danger from the fire. Then the Indians, seeing it would be impossible to dislodge him without some of them being killed, and probably having booty and victims in view in some other direction, withdrew.

The attack lasted fully six hours. Mr. Shoun fired, all told, twenty-three of his sixty-five cartridges. From the beginning, he carefully husbanded his ammunition. He continued in the hole over an hour after the Indians left, then he got out and hurried back to the ranch were [sic] *he arrived safely, but quite exhausted from his exertions.*

Mr. Morrison and a young man named Andrew Foster, the only two at the ranch, then returned to the scene of the desperate defense. No Indians were seen by them, but the statements of Mr. Shoun were fully corroborated by the general appearance of the spot. There was the hastily constructed fortification with the twenty-three cartridge shells strewn about, and the prairie burned all around for several hundred yards.

The Indians came from some Agency direct and must have started out on their murdering raid immediately after drawing rations, arms and ammunition.

This was demonstrated by the finding of the government sack containing a piece of pickled pork. And they were all armed with Winchester rifles. The night before the attack on Mr. Shoun, four men engaged in building cabins on ranches they had located on Elk Creek, about four miles below and northeast of Washta Spring, were driven away from their locations by a party of Indians supposed to be the same that attacked Shoun. It was the report of this affair that indeed convinced Mr. Shoun to deflect from the regular route to the Cheyenne Crossing and came up by the Washta Spring.

Later, from H.J. Wooley and Louis LaPlant, who came in last Monday from Washta Spring Ranch, we get the particulars of an attack on that place the day before—Sunday, the 22. About 7 o'clock in the morning, a party of Indians made their appearance, coming in from the direction of Elk Creek. They first rode around a number of cattle grazing nearby, and in plain view of the ranch, making a faint [sic] *of driving them off in order to draw out the inmates of the house, of which there were five men and one woman, the wife of Mr. LaPlant.*

This stratagem proving unsuccessful, the Indians then opened fire on the house, coming within three hundred yards, after which shots were exchanged in quick succession for probably three hours—Messrs Wooley, LaPlant, Shoun, Kelly and a teamster going outside and returning the Indians' fire from the corners of the house, behind which they would dodge at each discharge.

About 9 o'clock, two teams were spied coming in from Pierre, each charged of a driver, when LaPlant mounted his horse, and under a hot fire from the Indians while those who remained behind engaged from the house corners, rushed down the road and warned the incoming teamsters and helped to protect them into the ranch—where they arrived safely after having escaped many bullets fired at them.

The protective force at the ranch now numbered seven males and Mrs. LaPlant, who rendered valuable service carrying water and ammunition to the men.

The Indians then fired the prairie around the ranch, hoping to drive out the brave little garrison with fire, but the main wagon road being between them and the flames, this proved unsuccessful. The Indians continued firing and aiming at each one who would appear to view until about 3 o'clock in the afternoon when they withdrew, moving off in the direction of the Cheyenne River. About 9 o'clock the next morning, the 24, two companies of cavalry arrived from Fort Meade.

A few months later, in the spring of 1879, the Deadwood Trail at Dead Man's Creek was again the scene of a tragic gunfight. Among the bullwhackers who were tending their bull teams on the return trip back from Deadwood to Fort Pierre were James Layton Gilmore and Bicente Ortez, a native of Mexico. While unyoking their oxen, Gilmore and Ortez became engaged in an argument about a Deadwood dance hall girl. The discussion became more intense, and Gilmore shot Ortez four times—once in the shoulder and three times in the back as he was running away. Ortez died the next

This is all that remains of the headstone of Bicente Ortez, who was killed by bullwhacker James Gilmore in 1879 on a return trip from Deadwood. Ortez was killed when the two men had an argument over a Deadwood dance hall girl they had met. *Lonis Wendt collection.*

day. Meanwhile, other bullwhackers collected eighteen dollars among them and gave Gilmore a horse so he could leave camp and head for Fort Pierre. After resting and hiding out there for four or five days, Gilmore mounted up again and rode to Yankton. From there, he headed west, intending to find refuge on the Rosebud Reservation. He soon found work bullwhacking for the government and later managed a local saloon, where law enforcement officers arrested him.

On September 5, 1881, Gilmore was placed on trial. Two days later, a jury found him guilty of murder, but Gilmore's attorney appealed the decision. The Dakota Territorial Supreme Court agreed to consider the case but declined to change the guilty verdict, according to a *Black Hills Daily Times* report from May 19, 1879. Territorial governor Ordway stayed Gilmore's execution twice, but the gallows' trapdoor dropped on December 15, 1882, and Gilmore became the fourth of what would be the Dakota Territory's fifteen total executions. Frontier freighting was never easy or safe; perils were everywhere.

9

THE RAILROADS

The Pierre Daily *reports heavy shipments of freight to the hills. The Fred Evans line is transferring its teams to the Chadron route as rapidly as possible, but as considerable freight has been contracted for and ordered via Pierre, the old route will not be entirely abandoned before the last of September.*
—Black Hills Daily Times, *Deadwood, Dakota Territory, July 26, 1885*

Today, the railroad reaches the Black Hills. It is a day long hoped for and long looked for by the pioneers of this, the richest country in natural elements of wealth under the sun. Today is the time set for the celebration of the event of the coming of the railroad at Buffalo Gap, and a part of the celebration will be both new and novel.
—Black Hills Weekly Journal, *Rapid City, Dakota Territory, November 27, 1885*

From his high perch in the cab of the Fremont, Elkhorn and Missouri Valley locomotive, throttle master Ainsworth leaned out and waved postmaster George Boland to the front of his big, black engine that was still huffing and blowing steam after its run up from Chadron, Nebraska. Astride one of the new rails that was resting on level Black Hills pine ties, Buffalo Gap's Postmaster Boland took aim, swung a handmade mica hammer and drove a symbolic tin spike home. The dull thud of that ceremony may have lacked the rich, melodious ping of steel on steel, but it hammered Buffalo Gap into the history books as the place where the first

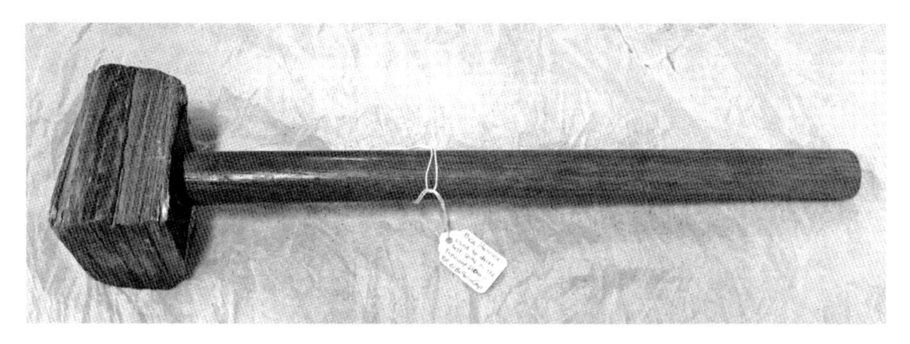

This mica hammer was used by George Boland to drive a ceremonial tin spike into the Fremont, Elkhorn and Missouri Valley Railroad line when it arrived in Buffalo Gap in late 1885. The Elkhorn was the first broad-gauge railway to enter the Black Hills. *Minnilusa Pioneer Museum, Rapid City.*

train chugged mightily into the long-isolated Black Hills. The Gappers liked the idea of using locally mined tin and mica for such an auspicious event, which not only marked the arrival of the first broad-gauge railroad to the hills but was also the beginning of the end of the bull trains that for the past decade had kept the hills alive. Gradually, the hills-bound goods and supplies were shipped on iron wheels rather than the big wooden ones that had been powered for so long by the lowly oxen over the Fort Pierre to Deadwood Trail.

The simple ceremony that had been planned by Postmaster Boland may have lacked the prominence and press of the gold spike that had been driven into the nation-spanning Union Pacific Railroad fifteen years earlier, but the Buffalo Gap celebrants and others who witnessed the event believed the train huffing into their little town on Beaver Creek would bring them fame and fortune. The town's residents imagined that Buffalo Gap would one day be the "Denver" of the hills. It was destined to become a busy and bustling Black Hills trade center, wrenching that honor from Deadwood and the new Rapid City. Prophetically, the bone-tired oxen of the Fred Evans line were, at the moment of the first train's arrival at Buffalo Gap, slowly plodding out of Deadwood with three faded green Murphy freight wagons. The oxen were among the last long haulers to stir the dust and manure in the streets of that legendary Black Hills town. Bull trains would, for a time, remain the hills' dray animals, performing short-haul deliveries, but the days of the bulls and bullwhackers on the Fort Pierre to Deadwood Trail were being ebbed into the mist of history.

It's logical to think that the railroads would have steamed into the Black Hills from the east, where both the Northwestern and Milwaukee lines were lounging on the eastern bank of the Missouri River, awaiting solutions to the Oceti Sakowin (Sioux) ownership of the land west of the river. But, then as now, government solutions were slow in coming, so it was necessary for a railroad associated with the Chicago and North Western line to skirt the far southwest corner of the Sioux reservation and head north to the hills from there.

Buffalo Gap was a natural gateway into the Black Hills and began as a sleepy stagecoach relay station that became known as the Beaver Creek Station. It was a little stopover on tranquil Beaver Creek, where the stage and freight trail coursed northward toward Rapid City, which was forty-five miles away, and had a branch that split toward Custer, which was just twenty-three miles to the west. The stage station and town were established in 1874 by George Boland and his brother Abe. The town was made to accommodate travelers, but it soon became a comfortable and lawless hangout for miscreants, four-flushers and malefactors, who would lounge about with moneyed travelers and those with gold, holsters flapping at their hips. At its peak, Buffalo Gap was home to about fifty smoky saloons and other places of raucous entertainment. A.K. Thomas, a telegrapher for the Elkhorn Railroad, was assigned to Buffalo Gap in early June 1886. His account of the town exists in the South Dakota History Collection, and in it, he says, "When I reached Buffalo Gap, and after reporting at the office, I walked to the end of the depot platform to take a look at the town. To me, it was the funniest looking village I ever had seen. The buildings, with one exception, were small, new and unpainted." Thomas was later transferred to the Rapid City station.

The natural Buffalo Gap is not far from the town; it twists and meanders through a narrow mountain ridgeline that encircles the hills. That ridgeline, also called a hogback, is like a geographical, tectonic ripple out from the hills. It forms a broad valley of reddish, iron-tinted soil between the ridge and the hills, separating the interior limestone plateau from the outer sandstone hogback. The Red Valley, also known as the Racetrack, has an inner core that is roughly eight thousand square miles in size; it was formed as the granite and gold in the earth was tilted, folded and twisted upward nearly two billion years ago. The gap gave the buffalo herds easy access to that five-mile-wide valley of red dirt. Other gaps in the ridgeline were located in Rapid City, Tilford, Sturgis and Spearfish. These locations were the doorways to the hills; they were welcoming sights to the trail-tired and dusty bull trains and other hoof-powered freight wagons and stagecoaches that were slogging along the last miles from Fort Pierre. The forty-mile path

Pennsylvanian and telegrapher A.K. Thomas (*far left*) was an employee of the Fremont, Elkhorn and Missouri Valley Railroad and was stationed at Buffalo Gap in 1885. The following year, he was assigned to accompany the first Elkhorn train to Rapid City. "Upon reaching Rapid City, we found the railroad had not yet built a depot, so we had to use an empty railcar." This photograph shows Thomas and others in front of the first telegraph office in Rapid City on July 5, 1886. *Minnilusa Historical Association, Rapid City.*

through the Racetrack from Buffalo Gap to the north wasn't well suited for railroad traffic, but at Rapid City, it leveled out and became the friendliest land for the Elkhorn that headed north to Sturgis, Spearfish and Belle Fourche. Because of the wide valley that spilled out onto the fertile, hay-rich prairie through the gap at Rapid City, the growing city was destined to become the trade center for the hills, snatching the esteemed title from the boisterous Deadwood and its bountiful gold fields.

A railroad into the hills had long been the hope and obvious need of those who had settled in the area to farm and ranch on the fertile prairie. During the early years of the gold rush, Deadwood was indeed the region's teeming epicenter; at the time, the future Rapid City was just a big hayfield with Rapid Creek running through it. The idea that Deadwood was the center of trade in the hills may have gotten a boost when, as early as 1878, Charles Atkins, an official of the Chicago and North Western Railroad, came to visit the town. He said he wanted to look over the town and test the mettle of the place, according to a *Black Hills Daily Times* report from

May 8, 1878. Deadwood civic and business leaders were extremely proud of the town and ecstatic over Atkins's visit. They viewed it as a bellwether of the community becoming the metropolis of the Black Hills. The locals referred to Deadwood as the "Denver of the Black Hills." Through the years, Deadwood's businessmen and women touted its prowess and potential. But when the Elkhorn Railroad chugged into Buffalo Gap in 1885, Deadwood residents scratched their heads as the Bolands and other Gappers dubbed their little town the "new Denver." Within seven or eight months of the Elkhorn rail line's arrival in Buffalo Gap and Rapid City, the old hay camp at the wide gap into the Racetrack truly became the "Denver." Once the railroad arrived, Rapid City remained the hills' major economic force.

In 1879 after the railroad leader's visit to Deadwood, the editor of the *Black Hills Daily Times*, when referring to the tremendous tonnage of freight that was being brought to Deadwood by bull trains and other hoofed transport, wondered, "We can't understand why a narrow gauge or even a broad gauge railroad wouldn't pay between the hills and either one of our Pacific connections." The editor was referring to the transcontinental Union Pacific Railroad in Nebraska, which was about 270 miles south of Deadwood, and the Northern Pacific Railroad, which was about 250 miles north of Deadwood. Neither railroad seemed willing to enter the fray to build a branch line to the isolated Black Hills. Their iron railroad tracks to the north and south of what became South Dakota were placed in their

Businesses were quickly established at Buffalo Gap in the extreme southwest corner of the Dakota Territory when the railroad arrived in August 1885. *South Dakota State Archives.*

respective locations because the southern half of Dakota Territory had the historic and geographical misfortune of being isolated between the nation's populated and wealthy eastern commercial and transportation centers, including Minneapolis, Chicago, Sioux City and Omaha.

As the growth of the population in the hills continued, the gold rush and the potential of a western frontier did gain some believers. Railroad barons hooked their thumbs in their vest pockets, leaned back in their office chairs, gazed at the gilded ceilings of their executive sleeper cars and considered the area's potential. In 1877, the Chicago North Western's managing director, Marvin Hughitt, envisioned the possibility of an east–west railroad that stretched across the southern half of the Dakota Territory and into the Black Hills. He ordered for track to be laid west from Tracy, Minnesota, and into the Eastern Dakota Territory (entering at the Hole in the Mountain east of Elkton in Brookings County) heading toward the Missouri River. Hughitt must have assumed that the warring Sioux dilemma would be solved by government action before his company's rails reached the Missouri.

Not to be outdone, the Milwaukee Railroad, which ran west, parallel to the Northwestern line in the Dakota Territory, set its sights on the tiny river city of Chamberlain, which was located downriver from Pierre. By 1880, both railroads had tracks to the east bank of the Missouri River but both were apprehensive about bridging the river due to the demands of the Sioux and the potential for hostilities. They were also apprehensive about going out past the river, because nothing much in the way of towns and homesteaders existed between the river and the Black Hills. It would be more than twenty-five years before the two railroads felt that conditions were favorable enough to make their moves into the Black Hills. From 1874 to 1886, those two railroads delivered goods and supplies partway to hills customers, but the last tired, dusty and slow leg still had to be done by oxen, horses, and mules traveling over the Fort Pierre to Deadwood Trail.

Meanwhile, the Chicago and North Western Railroad became a subsidiary of an eastern Nebraska short line, the Fremont, Elkhorn and Missouri Valley Railroad, which was often just called the Elkhorn or Cowboy line. There is no doubt that Hughitt had a hand bringing the Elkhorn Railroad to what became South Dakota from the south. And in 1883, survey crews and Elkhorn Railroad engineers began putting plans together to skirt the reservation lands and move into Dakota Territory and the Black Hills from the north in Chadron, Nebraska. Meanwhile, Buffalo Gap speculators and wheeler-dealers were biding their time, waiting for the train and the passengers who could afford the fare.

In early October 1885, the *Black Hills Weekly Journal* asked Abe Boland, the postmaster's brother, for news from Buffalo Gap. Abe told the newspaper that everything was "lively in that new burg." He continued, "A great many hard characters have flocked there from other places but are keeping quiet, and those interested in the town are determined that law and order shall be observed." Two weeks later, when Buffalo Gap's 240-pound town marshal, Archie Reardon, ordered well-known Black Hills troublemaker Charles Fugit to cease firing his pistol through the ceiling of a Gap saloon, Fugit defied the order and reached for his gun instead. But Marshal Reardon was quicker and shot Fugit twice, killing him. "The verdict of the best people at the Gap is that Fugit got his deserts," reported the *Weekly Journal* on October 30, 1885. Marshal Reardon, who would later become the mayor of nearby Hot Springs, was paid seventy-five dollars a month for keeping things quiet in Buffalo Gap. It was a big and dangerous job.

By 1885, Elkhorn Railroad construction workers were within fifteen miles of Buffalo Gap, busily working on land that was once claimed by Dick McCormick, according to the *Yankton Press and Dakotian*'s December 1, 1885 issue. The railroad had purchased the land from George Boland, who had divided his property around a depot site that was within a few yards of the old town of Buffalo Gap, and began selling lots. When Boland wasn't selling lots, he was planning an appropriate ceremony to welcome the first train into town. He asked the owners of the nearby tin mines to provide enough ore to fashion a mica mallet and tin spike for a spike-driving ceremony. A man named Mr. Cochran in Custer fabricated the ceremonial spike using tin from three of the eighteen nearby mines: the Raven, the Tin Mountain and the Dolphin. The *Buffalo Gap News* proudly proclaimed in its December 5, 1885 issue that, as the railroad neared the town, one hundred buildings popped up on land where there had been nothing but sagebrush just weeks earlier.

A few weeks before the Elkhorn's arrival in the new Buffalo Gap, the town's scandalous reputation was once again highlighted by a murder that was committed during a card game in one of the town's new saloons. Professional gambler John Donnan got into a dispute during a poker game when he shot a player that he claimed had been cheating. Charles Adams died instantly when he took a slug to the heart. Adams's brother-in-law, Doc Middleton, who was described by the *Black Hills Weekly Journal* as "the noted desperado," was informed by telegraph of the murder. Middleton left Gordon, Nebraska, on a fast horse and headed to Buffalo Gap for revenge. Upon his arrival, Middleton met the town marshal at the saloon where the killing had taken place and the fight and shooting were explained to him. Middleton relented, agreeing that his dead relative, whose body was lying in an adjoining room, was in the wrong. Middleton and Donnan then shook hands and sat down at the still bloodstained poker table, and as the *Journal* reported, "played a game for a good stake." All was once again quiet in Buffalo Gap.

Even as the Elkhorn Railroad drew nearer, Fred Evans and his bull trains remained busy hauling goods into the hills as supplies piled up from the trains that were chugging into the Chadron, Nebraska depot. On the day the Elkhorn finally pulled into Buffalo Gap, Evans's wagons had been on the road for four days, delivering thirty tons of Chadron freight to Deadwood. When they unloaded in Deadwood, the wagons were loaded back up with twenty tons of supplies for Rapid City and the Gap that were to be delivered on the return trip. That load included a shipment of Deadwood-brewed beer for Rapid City and furniture and dressed lumber for the buildings that were being constructed in Buffalo Gap, according to a *Black Hills Daily Times* report.

While the Evans bulls were delivering freight to the hills, a crowd cheered as the Elkhorn locomotive steamed into the Black Hills for the first time. The Deadwood newspaper reported that the train arrived at 10:30 a.m. "amid the huzzas and enthusiastic demonstrations generally of a very large assemblage." Aboard the train were more than fifty Elkhorn Railroad officials and guests, according to a report from the *Black Hills Daily Times*. Earlier that day, George Boland had sold thirty-five more lots, each starting at a price of $1,000, in his new town. One desirable location sold for what

This photograph from 1886 is said to be of the last bull train that left Fort Pierre for the Black Hills. *South Dakota State Archives.*

was then the amazing price of $1,350. As his sales ebbed, Boland sold three quarters of his interest in the remaining 120 acres for $10,000 to a group of five investors, including the Northwestern Freight line's agent in Deadwood, William Selbie, who was, without a doubt, anticipating the end to his bull train freighting job. The *Black Hills Weekly Journal* opined, "The railroad will bring people and capital, both of which are necessary. Hence, the coming of the railroad most clearly and distinctly marks a new epoch in the history of the hills."

On November 28, 1885, the day after the historic railroad entered Buffalo Gap, Evans's bull trains delivered 75,000 pounds of freight to Deadwood, with more expected to arrive the next day. The *Black Hills Daily Times* also reported that, between November 22 and November 28, 1885, the Evans line had lugged more than 100 tons of supplies into the hills from the Chadron train depot. With the arrival of the Elkhorn Railroad at Buffalo Gap, the Evans bull train freight wagons no longer had to slog off to Chadron; instead, they began operating out of the Gap, which meant that with good conditions, it would only take them a few days to make the trip. The Evans bull trains that hauled from the Gap to Rapid City in the early months of 1886 slowly passed by the Fremont, Elkhorn and Missouri Valley construction crews that were laying down steel to Rapid City. This also meant that, for a time, Buffalo Gap was a busy freighting center, just as Fort Pierre had been a decade before. But its days of sporting that title were quickly slipping away.

Even so, as 1886 began, the new *Buffalo Gap News* editorialized the town's success over the next nine months. In one article, they said, "There will be 27,000 visitors to Buffalo Gap, each of whom will expend at least ten dollars, making a pretty good aggregate of transient business." It wasn't long before a few of those assumed 27,000 visitors did stop by the new Buffalo Gap. Several couples from Rapid City came to town to take part in the grand opening of the Gap's new Flynn Hotel. A *Journal* story told of their visit. "They reported having enjoyed a very pleasant time, but while the dance was in progress, some thief or thieves stole a number of valuable wraps which they had left in the anteroom."

On February 8, 1886, a fire started in Buffalo Gap that burned many of the businesses in the little town of wooden comforts. At that time, the Boland side of Buffalo Gap had four blacksmith shops, three livery barns, seventeen hotels and cafes, twenty-three saloons and three Chinese laundries, in addition to a number of other busy shops. It is believed that the fire was the result of arson, but the culprit was never found. As the fire raged, the

Elkhorn Railroad was being set down near the beautifully sited town of Battle River, just a few miles south of Rapid City. Battle River soon became known as Hermosa, named after the Spanish word for "beautiful." The town was forced to rename itself because another Battle River already existed on the Elkhorn line in Nebraska.

The burgeoning town of Rapid City was soon to be the Elkhorn's next stop. According to the article "Railroads of the Black Hills," before the exact route to Rapid City was public, a rumor circulated that the rail line would be laid down three miles east of the city, passing by the business district. Around that time, the city donated a $15,000 bonus and thirty acres of good land for switching yards and a depot near the city's business center to the Elkhorn coffers.

Between seven and twelve thousand people turned out to welcome the Elkhorn into Rapid City, according to the *Rapid City Journal*. A group of well-wishers assembled at the Pennington County Courthouse and paraded to the train's arrival point. A ten-yoke bull train pulling a freight wagon that was decorated as a chariot trailed along the parade route as one of the last units in the long cavalcade of well-wishers. Exactly what that bull train was meant to symbolize is not known.

Locomotive engineer George A. Morton was at the controls as the train slowly rolled toward a depot site where the train's headquarters were to be built. The waiting crowd of thousands burst into cheers and applause as Morton's train gave a steamed sigh of relief and slowed to a halt. After the train's arrival, there were a number of welcoming speeches made, and the Seventh Cavalry Band from Fort Meade provided music between the long pontifications. When commenting on the railroad's arrival, the *Rapid City Journal* noted, "Thus, one by one, methods of the old times pass away and vanish before the progress of civilization as heralded by the railroad." After the Elkhorn's arrival in Rapid City—the new "Denver" of the hills—many small, independent freighters called it quits, fattened their cattle and put them on the sale block. So many oxen were put on the market that the prices for them dropped significantly. The remaining freighters, including the big freight companies, moved their operations to Rapid City and began hauling freight for the northern towns and camps in the hills. Fred Evans, the father of the Fort Pierre to Deadwood Trail, held on to the industry for a time, but according to a report from the *Black Hills Daily Times*, he soon began selling his warehouses that remained in many of the communities in the hills. Evans then put his bulls out to pasture on his farms in Iowa so they could be fattened and sold to meat packers. The Northwestern struggled on,

Late in the summer of 1886, the Fremont, Elkhorn and Missouri Valley Railroad built its first depot in Rapid City. *Minnilusa Historical Association, Rapid City.*

but a few years later, when Elkhorn Engine No. 43 struggled up the last steep grade into Deadwood, it was also sold.

By the early 1900s, both the Chicago and North Western line at Pierre and the Milwaukee Road at Chamberlain, which had been stymied on the east side of the Missouri River, finally took steps toward spanning the wide Missouri River. Within months, they were also serving the needs of the growing Black Hills community.

Fifty years after his travails on the old Fort Pierre to Deadwood Trail, former night-herder and bullwhacker Charley Zabel, who was by then living in his hometown of Sheboygan, Wisconsin, summed up what he and the thousands of other frontier freighters had accomplished in *Outdoor Life* magazine:

> *The last ox train has clattered its leisurely way over the old trail and vanished into Sunset Land, along with the buffalo, the longhorn and the Red Warriors. The stalwart men who made it possible to build towns and carry on commerce in the West are now few and scattered, but the part they played in this great pageant of the West will never be forgotten.*

APPENDIX A

"A WAGON TRAIN"

(Written for the *Deadwood Daily Times* on September 19, 1880)

White topped wagons, linked two and three,
Surrounding a camp near close of day,
Ox yokes scattered along the ground,
Show where each tired neck was unbound
Hungry cattle turned out to graze
Camp fires just beginning to blaze
Teamsters lie on the ground to rest.
And the sun just gone adown the west.

Cooks preparing the evening meal
As night's dark shadows round them steal
And after supper with pipes alight
And camp fires gleaning through the night
The teamsters lounge on the ground to smoke
And them their adventure, and laugh and joke
Ere wrapped in blankets they fall asleep
And leave the camp in the watchman's keep.

The tired cattle graze or sleep
While a herder the long night watches keep
And teamsters sleep where tents are spread
Or underneath their wagon bed
And thus the nighttime passes by

But when the day o'er spreads the sky
By earliest sunrays men are seen
Moving about the wagon train.

Fires are made and breakfast cooked
Cattle brought from the plain and yoked
And the herder's pony, with saddle on
And hanging rein stands in the sun
While among the freight the herder lies
With pillowless head and sleep closed eyes
Ne'er heeding the bustle of jostle or rattle
Nor loud voiced teamsters driving the cattle

Then the lines of teams with heavy loads
Almost block the mountain roads
And the wagons, two or three together
Are fastened one behind the other
And are drawn with heavy weight and rattle
By sixteen, eighteen or twenty cattle
All yoked and chained for a team together
And are driven by whips of braided leather.

Whose cruel lash, with many curves
Single out an ox that swerves
From allotted task and along its side
Oft leaves a red wound gaping wide
And where there's steep hills along the way,
They "double up" as teamsters say
Two teams are hitched to one team's load
And belted teamsters with hat rims broad

Wave along, loud lashes in the air,
And whip their teams and shout and swear
"Gee Bringham, come Beecher get along there Brin!"
Gee "Sellers," for the name of prominent men
Seems the teamster's delight and shouting loud
They urge the long line up the road
Till one lot of wagons is drawn to the crest
Then the teams go back to help the rest.

With white-topped wagons the road is lined
Through many a hill and valley wind
And the rash of each whip sounds like a shot
That causes a shudder at thought of the spot
Where the cruel lash struck
And winding down
The high toll road to a mining town
They almost fill the narrow street
With their piled up wagon loads of freight.

—Demetrius

APPENDIX B

BULLWHACKERS AND FREIGHTERS

The empty spaces in this section indicate that a name is unknown.

Allen, John "Jack"
Andrews, Bill
Apple, Morris
Arkansas, John
Ayes, Al
Barrett, Charley
Bates, ___
Bean Brothers
Beecher, George
Belcher, Jim
Bently, Lew
Benway, ___
Bernard, Polo
Billings, Joe
Black, Patsy
Blake, Steve
Blakely, Joseph
Borst, Harry L.
Borst, William
Brady, James
Bramble, Downer T.
Brinksworth, ___
Bronson, W.L.
Brown, Jesse
Buckingham, Emma
Buford, ___
Bullard, E.
Bullock, Seth
Callahan, James
Callaher, Mike
Callaher, Morris
Carpenter, ___
Collins, William
Craig, ___
Daugherty, "Honest John"
Davis, Charley
Day, James M.
Dean, Frank
Dean, George
Dennis, ___
Dickenson, ___
Dillon, John

Dixon, ___
Dorse, Andy
Dotson, "Captain"
Douglas, Tom B.
Doyle, John
DuFran, Charles
DuFran, Joe
Dunn, Dick
Dunning, Harry
Dupree, ___
Dyers, Charley
Edgar, Fred
Edgar, John
Elford, W.
Ellis, Kid
Erskine, Robert
Evans, Fred
Ferguson, ___
Ferris, ___
Fiman, ___
Flormann, Robert
Foley, ___
Forkenson, ___
Fosgate, Frank
Francis, Charles
Frost, Billy
Gallagher, ___
Gardner, C.V.
Gardner, William
Gee, Ben
Geigert, ___
Gilmore, James L.
Gordon, John
Hall, ___
Halloway, ___
Hannon, Frank
Hardy, ___
Harnett, Don
Harrison, John
Hart, ___
Hartley, ___
Hartsuff, ___
Hartzell, Lew
Hedges, ___
Hemphill, D.Z. "Tex"
Herskin, Balo
Hilger, Anson
Hilger, John
Holland, Mike
Hornick, John
Hurtzell, ___
Huxley, ___
Ingersoll, ___
Irish, J.G.
Jansen, Morris
Jepson, ___
Jewett, ___
Jobson, Matt
Johnson, H.
Johnson, William
Judson, H.C.
Kehlier, ___
Kelztemun, "Honest John"
Kent, M.B.
Killeher, Mike
Kirley, Joseph
Kirley, Will
Knight, J.W.
Knowlton, Zeke
Knutson, Armand
LaBlanc, Felix
Landeau, Maurice
LaPlant, Fred
LaPlant, George
LaPlant, John
LaPlant, Louis
Larive, Gideon
Larson, Peter

Lenhart, C.
Lyons, Dick
Man Called Billy
Mandan, ___
Martin, Mason
Mathison, Dick
Matlock, Jack
McCabe, G.
McCarthy, Frank
McCrossen, Barney
McHume, ___
McManus, Pete W.
Morine, Charles
Morris, Laban
Murphy, "Spud"
Newbanks, Noah
One-Armed Tom
Paine, D.A.
Parrish, L.E.
Parrott, ___
Pattenberg, John
Pattenburg, Joe
Pennell, ___
Perrelle, Joe
Philip, ___
Pierre, Ernest
Pitt, Joe
Pomeroy, Brick
Porter, ___
Porter, Jack
Powell, Dan
Powells, ___
Pratt, ___
Quinn, ___
Quinscoy (pronounced Casey), ___
Raymond, Red
Reed, S.D.
Reeders, ___
Rhoads, Frank
Rice, ___
Robinson, Joe
Roller, Nap
Runyan, J.S.
Ryan, John "Cheyenne Johnie"
Saddler, Edward
Sager, Charles
Sammis, Mart
Sammis, Oscar
Schofield, William
Seims, Peter
Selland, C.
Shaffer, ___
Shoemaker, ___
Shoun, M.P.
Shoun, Solomon
Sides, J.A.
Silverthorn, ___
Smith, Adam
Smith, S.P.
Snyder, C.
St. Clair, Billy
Stephens, Charley
Stuttering Dick
Sutley, Zack
Sweeney, Tom
Talbot, Dave
Thomas, "Smokey"
Timmins, Joe
Torkelson, ___
Turner, ___
Twomey, ___
Updegraff, "Shorty"
Vance, ___
Vollin, Isreal
Vollin, Joe
Vollin, Louis
Wahn, Dow
Waldron, ___

Walpole, ___
Wardner, Jim
Whitney, Frank
Willard, ___
Williams, Hank
Witcher, Eph
Witcher, Frank
Woods, Jim
Zabel, Charley

BIBLIOGRAPHY

Books

Bennett, Estelline. *Old Deadwood Days.* Reprint, Lincoln: University of Nebraska Press, 1982.

Brown, Jesse, and A.M. Willard. *Black Hills Trails: A History of the Struggles of the Pioneers in the Winning of the Black Hills.* Rapid City, SD: Rapid City Journal Company, 1924.

Cerney, Janice Brozik. *The Fort Pierre-Deadwood Gold Trail.* Self-published, instantpublisher.com, 2006.

Clark, Will Leach. *History of the Counties of Woodbury and Plymouth, Iowa: Including an Extended Sketch of Sioux City, Their Early Settlement and Progress to the Present Time, a Description of Their Historic and Interesting Localities, Sketches of the Townships, Cities and Villages, Portraits of Some of the Prominent Men, and Biographies of Many of the Representative Citizens.* Chicago: A. Warner & Co., 1890–91.

Forsee, Aylesa. *William Henry Jackson: Pioneer Photographer of the West.* New York: Viking Press, 1964.

Gardner, Mark L. *Wagons on the Santa Fe Trail 1822–1880.* Washington, D.C.: National Park Service Department of the Interior, 1997.

Hooker, William, F. *The Bullwhacker: Adventures of a Frontier Freighter.* Lincoln: University of Nebraska Press, 1988.

Hughes County History. Pierre: South Dakota Office of the Superintendent of Schools, 1937.

Jensen, Delwyn. *Deadwood–Fort Pierre Trail.* Pierre: State of South Dakota, 1989.

Karolevitz, Robert F. *Yankton: A Pioneer Past.* Aberdeen, SD: North Plains Press, 1972.

Kingsbury, George W. *History of Dakota Territory*. Chicago: S.J. Clarke Publishing, 1915.

Lavender, David. *The Great West.* Boston: Mariner Books, 2000.

McAllister, Linda (Kirley). *Gumbo Trails*. Self-published, 1957.

McDermott, John. *Gold Rush: The Black Hills Story*. Pierre: South Dakota Historical Society Press, 2001.

Meeker, Ezra. *The Ox Team: Or the Old Oregon Trail 1852–1906*. New York: self-published, 1907.

Morton, J., George L. Miller, and Albert Watkins. *Illustrated History of Nebraska: A History of Nebraska from the Earliest Explorations of the Trans-Mississippi Region, with Steel Engravings, Photogravures, Copper Plates, Maps, and Tables.* N.p.: Western Publishing and Engraving, 1907.

Nevin, David. *The Old West: The Expressman*. New York: Time-Life Books, 1974.

Parker, Watson. *Deadwood: The Golden Years*. Lincoln: University of Nebraska Press, 1981.

Robinson, Doane. *History of South Dakota*. Indianapolis: B.F. Bowen & Co., 1904.

Schell, Herbert S. *South Dakota: Its Beginnings and Growth*. Woodstock, GA: American Book Company, 1960.

Sneve, Virginia Driving Hawk. *South Dakota Geographic Place Names*. N.p.: Brevet Press, 1973.

South Dakota Historical Society. *Fort Pierre–Deadwood: Historical Atlas*. Pierre: South Dakota Historical Society, Cultural Heritage Center, 2008.

Tallent, Annie D. *The Black Hills, Or, the Last Hunting Ground of the Dakotahs: A Compete History of the Black Hills of Dakota, from Their First Invasion in 1874 to the Present Time*. St. Louis, MO: Nixon-Jones Printing Co., 1889.

Utley, Robert M. *Cavalier in Buckskin: George Armstrong Custer and the Western Military Frontier*. Rev. ed. Norman: University of Oklahoma Press, 2001.

Whitman, Sidney Edgerton. *The Troopers: Informal History of the Plains Cavalry 1865–1890*. New York: Hastings, 1962.

Newspapers

Bismarck Tribune
Black Hills Daily Times
Black Hills Pioneer
Black Hills Weekly Journal
Buffalo Gap News
Pierre Signal
Rapid City Journal
Sheboygan Press
Sioux City Journal
Sturgis Record
Yankton Press and Dakotian

Miscellaneous

Hodorff, Terri. "How Did Frederick Taft Evans Influence the Development of Communities in the Black Hills of South Dakota." Pennsylvania State University. citeseerx.ist.psu.edu.

South Dakota Historical Society Quarterly 17, no. 3–4 (1987).

South Dakota State Historical Collection

Zabel, Charley, with J. L. Beardsley. "Before the Railroad Came: The Story of the Life of an Overland Freighter on the Ft. Pierre–Deadwood Trail in the '70s." *Outdoor Life*, August/September 1933.

INDEX

T

U

V

W

Y

Z

ABOUT THE AUTHOR

Chuck Cecil is a native South Dakotan who currently lives in Brookings. He was born in Wessington Springs and grew up in Sturgis and Rapid City. He was an aerial photographer for the United States Navy during the Korean War. Later, he enrolled at South Dakota State University (SDSU) and earned bachelor's and master's degrees in journalism. After a decade in the newspaper business with the *Watertown Public Opinion* and the *Vermillion Plain Talk*, Cecil became an administrator at SDSU and served in various positions, including assistant to the president. He then established a chain of ten weekly newspapers in the Brookings and Sioux Falls area. Cecil retired in 2000 but has continued writing a weekly column for the *Brookings Register*, and he has written more than twenty books. He and his wife, Mary (Wilber) Cecil, have three children: Dan Cecil, a physician in Brookings, South Dakota; Matt Cecil, a dean at Minnesota State University in Mankato, Minnesota; and Amy Cecil Holm, an instructor at SDSU. Chuck and Mary also have five grandchildren.